VARIETIES OF FASCISM

Doctrines of Revolution
in the Twentieth Century

EUGEN WEBER

Professor of History
University of California
Los Angeles

AN ANVIL ORIGINAL

under the general editorship of

LOUIS L. SNYDER

D. VAN NOSTRAND COMPANY, INC.

PRINCETON, NEW JERSEY

TORONTO   LONDON

For Ida and Leo Gershoy

VAN NOSTRAND REGIONAL OFFICES:
New York, Chicago, San Francisco

D. VAN NOSTRAND COMPANY, LTD., *London*

D. VAN NOSTRAND COMPANY (Canada), LTD., *Toronto*

Published simultaneously in Canada by
D. VAN NOSTRAND COMPANY (Canada), LTD.

PRINTED IN THE UNITED STATES OF AMERICA

PREFACE

The word *Fascism* is widely used; the term *National Socialism* is increasingly current among the new regimes of Africa and the Near East. Many books have been published, and more are appearing, about Fascism in Italy and Nazism in Germany; but very few exist concerning similar phenomena between the wars, elsewhere. This study tries, not to *fill* the gap, but to suggest its existence. Much has been omitted in the account of tendencies which have a wider relevance in time and space than present superficial treatments indicate.

A general discussion of "fascist" ideas is, in the following pages, succeeded by short surveys of several Fascist or National Socialist movements in Europe between the last two wars, where we can note some of their similarities and differences. Since certain aspects recur in every movement, I have tried to indicate the particular characteristics of each and to show how they fit into a synthetic picture of the whole.

When dealing with a controversial subject—and one, moreover, which is far from closed—an author's views are no more than informed opinions, subject to interpretation and, eventually, correction. I have tried to keep prejudice out of the discussion, but have not thought that judgment was out of place. Such judgments, however, have been based to a large extent upon the very theories here examined and the aims expressed. In other words, my objectivity consists of taking Fascists and National Socialists at their word, whenever possible, and then seeing how far they were able to achieve their aims and in what measure the means they used contributed to their ends . . . or to their end.

There is no evidence I know that anybody knows better than anybody else what is good for him or what is good for others. There is, therefore, no particular reason why one should decide for others; or why not, provided he can force

3

or persuade them to accept his decisions. That is what
Fascists thought, determined to save men and nations even
against their will. Pragmatically, though (that is, by its own
standards), Fascism does not appear to work any better than
other methods of government, perhaps less constraining
though also less exciting. For the great tale of fumbling and
imperfection that history tells, here is a tentative report, to
join a great many others, of man's attempt to solve the
problems that he himself creates.

E. W.

TABLE OF CONTENTS

PART II—READINGS

Part I

FASCISMS AND NATIONAL SOCIALISMS

— 1 —

THE BACKGROUND

Origins. The 19th century had seen the heyday of liberalism, the rise of parliamentary and democratic institutions, the affirmation of private enterprise and individual liberty. The 20th century would be dominated by tendencies—collectivistic, authoritarian, antiparliamentary and antidemocratic—which stressed elitism against equality, activism and irrationalism against reason and contract, the organic community against the constitutional society.

All these tendencies had their roots in the 19th century, and even earlier—in the organic nationalism of a Rousseau for whom the national body, made up of the dead, the living, and those as yet unborn, ideally obeyed a general will best defined as a special revelation; in the thought of Hegel for whom the divine purpose revealed itself progressively in the history of nations; and in the romantic affirmation of the primacy of subjective passions, of instincts and of will, by which man was supposed to come nearest to nature, to reality, and to expressing his true self.

Forgotten for a time or, better still, adapted to the passion for science, positive knowledge, and rational activity which reigned over the century—especially over its second half—these concepts were revived in the 1890's and the early 1900's, when political and scientific disillusions swung the pendulum away from rationalism, away from the individualistic liberalism of the enfranchised, constitution-minded, free-trading middle classes. The prosperous, respectable, law-abiding bourgeoisie was decadent and corrupt, proclaimed Friedrich Nietzsche (1844-1900); only dynamic men, ruthless in thought and action, could save the race. Instincts are stronger than reason and closer to reality, suggested Henri Bergson (1859-1941). The individual is a product of the clan, taught the sociologist Emile Durkheim (1858-1917); collective consciousness has its own existence, prior to individual consciousness. And while these simplified ideas percolated from their books and lectures to a vaster public, new generations whom reigning rationalism bored stood by to welcome them. It was at this time that many of the ideas and institutions of the 19th century took a new shape and sometimes a new direction, their function and meaning changing here and there to answer the needs of another age.

Nationalism and Socialism had both been born or weaned in the 19th century. They were to be reaffirmed in the 20th, but in forms less humanitarian and less liberal and for motives different from their original ones. Both Nationalism and Socialism had first appeared as liberating movements. In the shape they assumed during the 1900's, they would be less liberating than constricting. Where once they had expressed the real needs and real resentments of men oppressed, exploited, and insecure, now they were tapped as myths—potentially powerful invocations addressed to tendencies and awarenesses that they themselves had been instrumental in creating over the past century. And, while we know that both Nationalism and Socialism were potent as separate—generally antagonistic —creeds, both also contributed to those new phenomena peculiar to our age that we call Fascism or National Socialism.

Neither Fascism nor National Socialism has been investigated thoroughly, although both are highly characteristic of our time: a time in which theory and activism, pragmatic violence, and idealistic ruthlessness masquerading as positivism dominate or threaten all societies. The peculiar combination of Nationalism and Socialism seems to answer the needs of a great many states, even though this is not always explicitly acknowledged or self-conscious.

The study of Fascist and National Socialist phenomena has suffered from several serious drawbacks: both movements expressed themselves in actions and statements which repelled serious scholars as they repelled any humane person; both movements were defeated in circumstances which make an unprejudiced approach difficult; and both movements, once defeated, were temporarily dismissed as having no further immediate significance, except of a purely historical order—and that could wait. Meanwhile, the fiery trail of Fascism and Nazism, driving like destructive comets through Italian and German history, had drawn all eyes to these two countries, leaving little attention for similar phenomena elsewhere.

Because neither Fascism nor National Socialism has been thoroughly analyzed, we lack sound definitions of either and frequently confuse the two. Only the ignorant still think that Socialism and Communism, much though they have in common, are one and the same thing. But even serious scholars are liable to refer to "German Fascism," and to use Fascism and National Socialism interchangeably. True, the activity of German National Socialists involved the violent methods which we associate with Fascism; but violence is not the prerogative of either of these movements, and we shall see that there are fundamental differences between them which might help us to reach a new classification.

Today, terms like Nazi or Fascist, especially the latter, have become adjectives used in a sense that is only vaguely descriptive and generally pejorative. Their purpose is often to give a dog a bad name, their use seldom exact: Franco is a Fascist, Perón was a Fascist, Pétain was a Fascist, but Churchill, Eisenhower, and de Gaulle may be Fascists too (depending upon who is talking), and so may Tito. Yet these phenomena, crucial to our time, are not only part of the history of the past, but of the present and the future as well. Fascism and National Socialism have to be analyzed and defined so as to establish in what they are alike and in what they differ, to discover what makes them start and what makes them tick, to understand to whom they appeal, why, and by what means.

Theory and Practice. There are two levels on which political ideas and political movements operate: theory and

practice. Although we have been fascinated by Fascist practice in Italy and Nazi practice under Hitler, we have paid
relatively little attention to their theory and even less to
evidence from other countries where similar movements
and similar doctrines flourished. And yet the essence of
certain doctrines is to be found in their expression when
they have not yet "arrived": in the period of formulation,
controversy, soap box oratory, and obscure pamphleteer-
ing; in the discussions and exegeses of the movement's
theorists, whose definitions and formulas may be removed
from the brutal realities of the political struggle, but are
accepted—and honored in the breach if not in the observ-
ance. The struggle to reach or to maintain power involves
a political movement in hedging, compromise, back-pedal-
ing, and all the complications which follow when theory
has to be connected with practice, when it has to be adapted
to the concrete realities of traditional politics and political
maneuver. It is the theories, the doctrines, the ideologies
of Fascism and National Socialism—and the attempts to
carry these into practice—that will be considered in the
following pages.

It has been held that National Socialist doctrine is of no
importance, because Hitler came to power in spite of it
and, once in power, did not apply it—at least, not the
Socialist part. This kind of argument does not prevent us
from studying Marxist or Leninist doctrine, even though
the Bolshevik revolution of 1917 went counter to then-
existing theories, and though Bolshevik practice since that
time has only partially conformed to it. The aspect of
Communism changes according to whether it is practiced
by Russians, Serbo-Croats, or Chinese; but we can study
the theory of Communism and learn a good deal from it.
In the United States, too, Republicans and Democrats are
elected to office having expressed a variety of ideas and
made a variety of promises, although everyone accepts as
a fact of life that platforms are made to run on, not to
stand on. Nevertheless, political scientists know very well
that platforms and ideologies are significant, partly because
they do tell us something about what the candidate and his
party think (or would like to think, or would like the
public to think they think) and partly because they reflect

a public: the issues this public is likely to be affected by, to vote for, or in some way support.

The argument is current that Fascist manifestoes or the program of the National Socialist German Workers' Party are meaningless because they were never really carried out. In fact, such statements were acted upon to quite a surprising extent. Even if they had not been, we should still learn a good deal by examining them, especially if we compare them to similar programs or doctrines evolved by movements in other countries and, perhaps, in other circumstances.

Earlier Movements. Movements of a National Socialist nature are not peculiar to the 20th century. F. L. Schumann, in his book *The Nazi Dictatorship* (New York, 1935), suggests that the idea, if not the name, can be traced back to the German Romantics, to the autarkic economist Friedrich List (1789-1846), and also to Ferdinand Lassalle (1825-1864), the German-Jewish Socialist leader who was a contemporary of Bismarck. Fifteen years before Schumann's study, in a book published just after the First World War, *Prussianism and Socialism,* Oswald Spengler had argued that the prototype of the modern Socialist state is to be found in the ideas of Frederick the Great, founder of the perfected Prussian bureaucracy. It is equally possible to trace the pattern of the planned totalitarian society back to Plato's *Republic,* and the Fascist mentality to the turbulent, unscrupulous Callicles who appears in another Platonic dialogue, *Gorgias.*

Even if we try to narrow things down, we shall find self-asserted National Socialists rampant as far back as 70 years ago. In 1896, Friedrich Naumann (1860-1919), the great economist of the Wilhelmian era, tried to organize what he called a National-Social Party. Something like it already existed in Austria, where it was called the German Workers' Party and where, in 1896, its leader Karl Lueger became Mayor of Vienna, a position he retained until 1910. During this time he carried out what by all accounts was a most thorough and efficient program of municipal Socialism and also provided the basic inspiration of a young drifter called Adolf Hitler (1889-1945), who sometimes sold the party paper in the street. In 1918, Lueger's move-

ment would change its name to the German National
Socialist Party.

In France, meanwhile, in the same year that Lueger became Mayor of Vienna, a typical nationalist buccaneer was
being given a lavish funeral in the Cathedral of Notre
Dame, with the Archbishop of Paris officiating and Maurice
Barrès, in his funeral oration, asserting that the Marquis
de Morès, whose memory they had gathered to honor, had
been both nationalist and socialist. As for himself, said
Barrès (1862-1923), he also liked to insist on the intimate
union of nationalist and socialist ideas.

Barrès had already expressed this view in a periodical,
La Cocarde, where extreme nationalists collaborated with
extreme syndicalists. The review only lasted from 1894 to
1895, but while it lasted, it preached the gospel of social
revolution "whose accomplishment no power can henceforth prevent," it lambasted the established order, and it
attacked with particular vigor the capitalist system that
throve upon it. One of Barrès's admirers considered that
the review "was exactly socialist in that it led a relentless
struggle against economic liberalism, and called for the
organization of labor and the suppression of the proletariat,
that is to say its integration in society." This is not what
most Socialists would recognize as Socialism, but there are
a great many variants of Socialism, and we shall see that
this is the one which Fascists and National Socialists
favor. It was this that Barrès himself had in mind; and
when in 1898 he stood for election in Nancy, capital of
his native Lorraine, his program was headed "Nationalism,
Protectionism and Socialism," and his supporters gathered
in the Republican Socialist Nationalist Committee.

They did not get very far; but the label was attractive.
It was revived a few years later by Pierre Bietry, a dissident
trade-union leader who tried to gather in a Socialist National Party the working-class opposition to the doctrinaire
policies of the French Confederation of Labor (C.G.T.).
Meanwhile, the idea itself was bringing young intellectuals
together in a number of groups and reviews in which the
nationalist disciples of Charles Maurras (1868-1952)
worked together with the revolutionary syndicalist disciples
of Georges Sorel (1857-1922). Maurras, a convinced
royalist, had built up a movement—the *Action Française*

—whose purpose was to restore the monarchy, a sense of order, hierarchy, and discipline in French political and intellectual life. Sorel, on the other hand, who came from the Republican left, was seeking to renovate current social revolutionary ideas and adapt them to the conditions of the 20th century. At first sight, no more different points of view could be conceived. Both men, however, agreed in their criticism of the existing political, economic, and social order, of parliaments, democracy, liberalism, and capitalism, and both despised the existing parties of the Right and Left and their leadership for their conservative, stick-in-the-mud policies.

The brief flirtation did not go far, and its inspiration finally foundered in the great war (1914-1918) in which most of the young enthusiasts lost their lives. But it represented a tendency, perhaps a need, which has persisted until our own day. In the next 30 years, more than a score of groups and movements appeared in France alone, bearing titles like National Syndicalists, Monarchist Socialists, National Proletarians, Revolutionary Patriots, or simply National Socialists.

Even if we consider that the combination of these supposedly antagonistic ideologies amounted to little, in movements that were often insignificant and generally short-lived, the question remains why people should be so interested in the conjunction of Nationalism and Socialism as to go on suggesting it, and what it was that made this conjunction seem relevant to so many about this time. The hint of an answer may be found in Clouard's words about the *Cocarde's* "relentless struggle against economic liberalism."

Antiliberalism. All opposition movements of the 20th century seem to have in common this opposition to a liberalism defined on the economic plane as the application of competitive *laissez-faire* and on the political plane as the individualistic counterpart of *laissez-faire* which allows *particular* interests to assert themselves at the expense of the social whole. In opposing individualism and the apparently chaotic conclusions of private enterprise, their critics rediscover collectivism. On such grounds, they find that they have more in common with Socialists (though not with Social-Democrats) than with more conservative groups and

that it might be convenient to adopt some of their ideas
or even enter into an alliance with them.

This approach was the basis of German National Communism, whose possibilities impressed quite a number of
people in the Weimar Republic of 1919 and the early
1920's. While the Communist, Karl Radek, was interned in
the Berlin prison of Moabit, he was visited among others
by Baron Eugen von Reibnitz, a colleague of Marshal
Ludendorff in the Cadet Corps and "the champion in officers' circles, not only of alliance with Soviet Russia, but
of the so-called peaceful revolution. Reibnitz was of the
opinion that the central task of restoring the productive
forces of Germany was insoluble without the nationalization of industry and without factory committees." The great
Walter Rathenau, himself a representative of vast industrial
interests, and another visitor in what Professor E. H. Carr
has called "Radek's Political Salon," admitted that there
could be no return to the old capitalist order. A new society,
in which capitalism, the right of inheritance, the old social
categories, would disappear, in which the most intelligent
and the strongest would be the leaders, should be created
by the working class under the leadership of an aristocracy
of intellect which would closely resemble Dr. Rathenau
himself. In another vein, 15 years later, one of France's
most influential economic journalists argued that socialist
opposition to liberal individualism attempts to provide the
kind of collective awareness which liberal capitalism lacks,
and that the only hope of neutralizing the socialist appeal
lay in the production of a collective and unifying ideology
that could match it.

A good statement of this point of view may be found in
a book published in Paris in 1943, during the German
occupation, entitled *Theses for the National Revolution*.
"The capitalist system," it declares, "is dominated by
[*private*] profit. The capitalist age is characterized by selfishness. . . . In its present form, capitalism is condemned to
disappear because it has not associated the majority of
producers to the distributive process."

This kind of awareness, this kind of scruple, had not
played a very significant role in the 19th-century middle-
class thought—especially not after 1848. The first to discover the drawbacks of liberalism had been those well-in-

tentioned members of the middle and upper classes whose reason, conscience, or sensibilities had been shocked by the sufferings of the urban poor. Their yearnings for a better organized society would survive as one of the strands of our story. More concrete political action could be expected from those who first felt the ill effects of liberal free enterprise: that is, the propertyless workers. Particularly in the great and growing cities of Western Europe, industrialization created a class of permanent wage earners devoid of property and therefore not commited to individualistic principles. Such people were amenable to collectivistic arguments, first of a nationalistic, then of a socialistic sort. Adam Smith (1723-1790) had argued that men further the common interest when they pursue their own interests with enlightened selfishness. This argument, however, was not convincing to propertyless wage earners whom the system exploited without satisfying. They were not persuaded that what is good for General Motors is good for the nation; or perhaps they felt that they were not really full members of this kind of nation.

Tariffs, commercial competition, threats of war on the one hand; the growing effectiveness of syndicalist organization and its more active participation in national and international politics on the other—all emphasized the superior effectiveness of groups over unorganized individuals. Meanwhile, the middle classes were facing problems of their own. Where earlier opportunities had not been lacking for the small entrepreneur to set up in business, make money, and rise in the social scale, now big business, big capital, growing labor, taxing and interfering states, were all squeezing him out of business. And so, beginning in the late 19th century, certain sections of the middle classes, threatened especially by the encroachments and the competition of great capitalist enterprises, began to consider their danger and to welcome or, at least, to heed collectivistic doctrines which stressed the need to regulate the workings of capital in order to protect the people (in this occurrence themselves) from private exploitation.

First, they resented the kind of unregulated speculation that made unwitting investors lose their savings in spectacular crashes; then they came to fear the competition of large department stores, chain stores, and trusts (those

"heejous monshthers" that Mr. Dooley talked about). It
was no longer enough for a man to work hard, save, and
thrive: a big combine could put him out of business, his
savings might disappear overnight, because of obscure
machinations he ignored; his farm might become useless
because people halfway across the world could produce
more wheat and fatter sheep and ship them to his country
and still undersell him. This seemed sheer chaos to the
little man, and it was easy to persuade him that the economic developments which were endangering and eliminating small and medium enterprises, and which affected farmers as well, were typical of a system that was intrinsically
anarchic.

In a sense that was true. But economic anarchy had gone
unnoticed as long as its possibilities had helped rather than
hindered the making of money. Now, liberal economics
started to look threatening to a number of people who
had in the past benefited from it; and, by a natural equation, it became connected in many minds with liberal
politics, similarly competitive and similarly anarchic, which
had better be replaced (the argument began to be heard)
by a more reliable order: restrictive, protective, controlling
private enterprise in order to protect it, not to destroy it.

Naturally, most of these people did not know how to
formulate their resentments and their claims, and their
plight did not attract much attention from the theorists
until the twenties and the thirties when it became really
widespread and manifest. But this seems to be the basis
of the right-wing spectrum noticeable during the last half-
century, and also the basis of differences of orientation to
be found within the so-called Right: the difference between
conservative and radical tendencies. Those who benefited
from the established order were firmly conservative, and
so were some of the small, threatened property owners.
But the mass of the latter, together with those whom the
system stripped of the security and the income which they
once enjoyed, would oscillate between variants of radicalism, all of which repudiated liberalism and capitalism, some
envisaging a return to a sort of Jeffersonian golden age,
while others wanted to forge ahead, through revolution, to
a new collectivistic social order.

Insofar as they all suspected or feared the class-covetousness of Socialist claims and ignored the class character of their own resentments, these people were united in opposition to conventional Socialism and Communism. They were united, too, by a common belief in the national entity and in the value of national definition—a belief which the Marxists traditionally denied or, at least, played down. Nationalism was going to furnish the ideological basis on which otherwise divergent sections of the Right would join in temporary alliances, and also the inspiration for doctrines of reform which the less conservative sections could accept, adopt, and follow.

— 2 —

NATIONALISM

Utopia and Myth. To use two words dear to the heart of Georges Sorel, Nationalist ideology appears in modern times both as utopia and as myth. The utopia, Sorel tells us, is the imaginative construction of a possible future, which implies the partial, progressive realization of the things it describes. A myth, on the contrary, is something unreal, whose very unreality makes it possible to keep up a violent, intransigent, doctrinaire position. To be politically effective over a long period of time, an ideology must combine these two characteristics. It has to be concretely applicable and effective, yet it must have a certain ultimate character, which acts as a sort of ideal carrot, intangible, inspiring—perhaps the more inspiring for being intangible.

The need for such a creed is not felt in periods of social and moral stability when people operate in a familiar world, in terms of familiar and unquestioned institutions, authorities, and customs. It is when things change rapidly, when customary patterns break down, when social order collapses and existing values begin to be questioned, that

radical inspirational creeds not only flourish but mushroom
—as mystery religions did in the Hellenistic world and
again at the beginning of the Christian era, in epochs of
instability, insecurity, and flux.

All such creeds combine the qualities of utopia and myth
that Sorel regarded so highly. Students of religion have
discussed how close Christianity came to other mystery
religions of the Hellenistic world, which also stressed ideas
of sin and redemption, salvation and a savior. Nationalism,
too, has many things in common with other great religions
of its time: with the 18th-century belief that man can conceive and build the good society according to a rational
pattern, with the romantic belief in society as an organic
whole, with the Darwinian ideas of natural selection, and
finally and most specifically, with the social and collectivistic ideas based on all of these, which affirm, as nationalists also like to do, that no man is an island entire
of itself.

Frequently confused with expansionism, imperialism, or
aggression, Nationalism is not necessarily connected with
any of these. The feudal lord who raids or annexes the land
of another lord is not a nationalist. The Crusaders or the
Spanish adventurers who clutched at new lands for profit
and for faith were not nationalists. Louis XIV was not a
nationalist when he annexed some neighboring prince's
territory for his own glory or profit. And even Bismarck,
uniting a large part of Germany under Prussian sway,
flouted the dreams of German nationalists for the sake of
the Hohenzollern family and the Prussian State which he
served.

Nationalism, in other words, is less a policy than an idea:
it is the acute, ideological form of normal everyday patriotism and of a new awareness grounded in the growth of
national states throughout the early modern period. Where
patriotism arises directly from simple emotions connected
with people and places that we know and care for immediately, Nationalism uses intellectual arguments based
on more sophisticated ideas like tradition, history, language,
and race; it argues a wider community and a common
destiny which are not immediately perceptible but whose
traces can be found in the past, whose reality can be de-

monstrated in the present, and whose implications have to be worked out in the future.

Historical Origins. Like so many other phenomena of modern history, this sort of Nationalism draws much of its impetus and ideology from the French Revolution of 1789. Give or take a generation, most of the attitudes that we recognize as nationalistic appear in the late 18th century: awareness and exploration of a peculiar common past and a similar present culture; emphasis of the group and the community in which the individual fulfills himself; insistence on a common interest and a common responsibility which makes the individual part of the group in a way he had never been before; finally, the growing identity between the nation and the state—between the political and administrative machine on the one hand, and the cultural community on the other—which would provide nation-states with an impetus that marks the whole 19th century.

Not all of these concepts developed at once, and not all of them appeared together. But all implied a sense of community that had not existed in a Christian world where men were truly one in God alone; or in an "enlightened," reasonable world where individual men could be united only by contract or by force; or in existing monarchies which were visualized as the property of their rulers, and where the state was simply the managing board of a vast private enterprise.

There could be devoted paternalism on the one hand, filial loyalty and obedience on the other, but this did not really involve the king's subjects in the king's affairs. There could be the reluctant contractual agreements of John Locke, or the enlightened despotism of Frederick the Great, but they were all limited, utilitarian arrangements which left the individual essentially free of responsibility in the community. Perhaps the Christian religion came closest to suggesting a unity among men. But even Christian unity was not fundamental, because, really, men were all striving individually toward their personal salvation; and even this superficial community broke down in the 16th century. By the 18th century, Christianity no longer provided a serious cultural inspiration. It was still a cultural reality; it was still a social force; but thinking men did not look toward it to find solutions for their problems.

And so, Nationalism appears as a sort of whistling in the dark. There is safety in numbers; and it is not surprising to find anxious, disoriented men gathering together to draw confidence and a feeling of identity from each other's presence. They had something to worry *about*. The 18th century was the time when God died, to be replaced by a watchmaker. It was the time when rulers were cut down to size, as a preliminary to more radical disseverments. Habit and custom, the essential ingredients of social cement, were cracking all over the West. Finally, the principle of monarchy itself was called into question, and the principle of property along with it, because if you take a king's lands away you are depriving him of his property, and if you challenge a king's right to rule his lands you challenge any man's right over his property.

People worried and wondered where all this was going to stop, where they could find a new principle, a new authority to take the place of the fallen ones. The new principle appeared in the idea of the nation. The soldiers of the old regime had gone into battle shouting "Long live the King"; the soldiers of the revolution went into battle shouting "Long live the Nation." Here was the superior entity for which they were ready to lay down their lives: the totality of Frenchmen, the nation, a community that was both real and ideal. And here we come to a basic characteristic of European Nationalism, which has not been sufficiently noticed—its collectivistic nature.

Certain national ideas that we can trace back during the century that preceded the French Revolution had been formulated with a different end in view. When in 1688 the English dispossessed James II of his crown and handed it over to William of Orange, this same threat to the principle of property had arisen. John Locke had answered the threat by arguing, not that the community is superior to the individual, but that the individual and his property interests are anterior to the community and hence basic to it. "The great and chief end of men uniting into commonwealths and putting themselves under government," wrote Locke, "is the preservation of their property." Locke's *Two Treatises on Government* emphasized that the individual—his liberty, his dignity, his property, his happiness

—must always be the basic element of all social life even within the state; this principle presided over the British philosophy of politics and over its great offspring in North America.

This kind of view, which is essentially conservative (whatever its revolutionary implications or rationalizations might be), was not suited to the revolutionary situation that Europe was facing after 1789. The theory that men joined in a community for the sake of their particular convenience (mostly of a material kind) was of no use to states in crisis or to revolutionaries who set out to challenge vested interests (also mostly of a material kind). Something more radical was called for to match their needs, and this would be the collectivistic nationalism with which the modern period is better acquainted.

Collectivistic Nationalism. A doctrine which stresses the national community is rich in collectivistic implications to begin with. The king's pleasure was replaced by the general will; the arbitrary operation of hierarchy and privilege was replaced by equality before the law; the state had been the property of the prince: now the nation became the common property of its citizens. The development of Jacobin thought in the days of Robespierre and Saint-Just shows these ideas in action: the nation and the people are one, said the Jacobins. For the benefit of both nation and people, the representatives of this totality of the general will can dispose of individuals and of property because both individuals and property exist only in function of the common good.

Robespierre and Saint-Just came to a bad end (as men of principle so very often do), but the ideas persisted. Obviously, if the nation was the highest good, if it was the worldly incarnation of the divine spirit at work in history, if it was an absolute necessity for the well-being and the self-fulfillment of its citizens, then its interest must be supreme; no petty rights like property and individual liberty could be set up against it, because property, individual liberty, and cultural self-expression existed only in and through the nation. The part could never be greater than the whole, and it might quite properly be subordinated and sacrificed to the interests of the whole.

These very ruthless implications were not developed at

once. In 1792, the National Convention meeting in Paris had declared "in the name of the French people that it will accord fraternity and assistance to all peoples who shall wish to recover their liberty." But liberation turned to occupation (as it often does), and the armies of the Republic were succeeded by the armies of the Empire, and these, in turn, by a series of reactionary regimes. During this time, the confident, liberating Nationalism (which envisaged the national collectivity as part of a vaster order, an order where friction and war would be eliminated by national self-determination), turned into the sort of Nationalism for which national interests have to be affirmed at the expense of others.

In 1792 and in 1848, nationalists were still humanistic and universalistic: Italians, Poles, or Frenchmen would not only save themselves, but they would save the world. Affirming their right to freedom, they affirmed the same right for others, too. By 1870, let alone by 1918, they had all become self-assertive to the point of aggression. The nationalist ideology, once it had been accepted, had taken up the narrow opportunism of traditional politics. In other words, where Nationalism captured the state, it was in turn captured by the state; and it was used (consciously or not) to rationalize actions and policies which were not specifically nationalistic. The relations between nationalists in different countries were basically changed as soon as any of them graduated from mere theory to real state power. When they became bureaucrats and politicians, the nationalists assumed the implications and the responsibilities of economies and policies that were based not on cooperation, but on competition. Their ideology became a new flag to wave over the old-fashioned armies of opportunistic power politics.

Economic Factors. Something else happened to complicate the problems and the nature of Nationalism. Just when its ideology had established itself and pervaded the public mind, Nationalism had to cope with rapid changes that were taking place in the scale of economic and industrial activity. At the turn of the 18th to the 19th century, Nationalism had been a practical innovation. The national state had been an improvement over the congeries of autonomous units it replaced: it offered people more scope and a wider area of action. But by the end of the 19th century, the needs and the pressures of a vastly more productive, more integrated, more complex economy were already finding this scope too narrow. The nation as an economic unit was being involved in a much vaster world market. A new kind of collectivism—world collectivism—pressed in upon the more limited—national—one. And Nationalism had to become defensive and to resist the intrusion of new forces and new ideas—just because the expansive pressures of modern industry were making it aggressive and because the self-sufficient nation-state that had been such an advance only a little while before was becoming less viable and also more involved and more vulnerable in the cat's cradle of modern world economy.

These same expansive forces, which accentuated the doctrinal contradictions within Nationalism, also generated a new doctrinal challenge outside it—Socialism, which appears toward the end of the 19th century as the opponent and the foil of Nationalism, but which is actually the product of the same assumptions that were part of Nationalism itself.

In 1789, men had set out to organize their world according to their own laws and not to those of some external order. To do this, they had transferred political thought and action from the private to the collective level; the first stage of this revolution had been political. But it did not take long before claims were advanced for a further revolution, a social revolution, which would serve more than a limited minority of the middle class: a revolution of and for the whole people, which would set up a new economic and social order and not just a new form of government, which would (in other words) go further toward fulfilling the logical conclusions of the principles of 1789.

By the end of the 19th century these views were identified with Socialism. But they could just as easily be identified with Nationalism. If they were not, it is because the connection between Nationalism and collectivism had in the meantime been lost from sight. And this had happened for a very practical reason: as the middle classes achieved their political objectives in some kind of national and constitutional order, and as they attained their economic objectives by gaining opportunity and prosperity and security, the old slogans of revolutionary and collectivistic self-determination did not suit them any more. These people believed in the nation, and they believed in the general will; but they also believed in property—and property was being challenged by the ideas of the Socialists.

How were they going to reconcile the new reality and the old doctrine? How were they going to reconcile the collectivistic implications of what they believed with the collectivistic demands of what they withstood? How were they going to join—or openly join—the camp of established order, which they had opposed for so long? There was the problem: a middle class, which had been identified with the party of movement, achieves its objectives and begins to appreciate the *status quo*. But while its interests call for stability, its ideology remains an ideology of movement and reform. How can it become a party of order and yet continue to flatter itself that it still represents movement and progress? The way to do so was to emphasize that part of its doctrine whose dynamism did not threaten its interests. Here nationalism was useful: against the divisive doctrines of class war, the erstwhile revolutionaries (now replete) proclaimed the old Jacobin doctrine of national unity; against the subversive doctrines of Socialist internationalism, they reaffirmed the reality of the nation in arms, facing a foreign foe. When they had persuaded themselves that this is what Nationalism means, they were able to march into the conservative camp—the camp of property and the *status quo*—with a clear conscience. For a while, after the turn of the century, Nationalism was going to provide the slogans of the respectable Right against the collectivistic ideas of the subversive Left. This was paradoxical, because Nationalism had been the first to challenge property rights for the sake of a superior interest; now it was mobilized to defend property and the established order that went with it.

Conjunction of Right and Left. Under the surface, all sorts of ferments were working, both on the Right and on the Left. Many Socialist leaders were patriotic at heart. They mouthed the slogans of international working-class unity, they called on the workers of the world to unite against their class enemies, but actually they feared the competition of foreign labor and hated the national enemy much more than the class enemy. This was best shown in

1914, when, on the outbreak of war, the workers abandoned class for national resentments and rallied like everybody else to the cause of the Fatherland.

At the same time, however, many right-wing Nationalist leaders were social radicals, and they had their own ideas about what Nationalism meant. The conservative Right, which was glad enough to use the slogans of Nationalism, was too conservative to consider the more radical implications of the doctrine. And this was going to bring about a split in the Right—between non-doctrinaire conservatives on the one hand, and radical doctrinaires on the other—a split hidden from sight much of the time by the common use of nationalist slogans, but which we can now trace, in Germany and Austria and France, right back to the end of the 19th century.

Men like Maurice Barrès in France described themselves as National Socialists. They realized that national unity implied social justice, that national power implied the planned use of national resources, that national harmony might mean the equalization or the redistribution of wealth and opportunity and economic power. Being doctrinaire, they were willing to be ruthless. Being intellectuals, they did not feel the need to maintain the established order at all costs. Putting the nation first and property second, they found that their theories were leading them toward Jacobinism—even while the official left-wing heirs of the Jacobins were moving in the opposite direction.

These national-collectivist ideas were going to be put into practice during the First World War: planning, direction, compulsion, taxation. The nations mobilized their resources, regardless of the property rights that conservative Nationalism was supposed to defend. When the war ended and the Jacobin measures were allowed to lapse, an ideological residue remained: when you are hard pressed, you can mobilize the nation. And the first to take this advice was a heretical Socialist, Mussolini.

THE RISE OF FASCISM

Mussolini's Movement. A leading figure in the Italian Socialist movement and editor of the party paper, Benito Mussolini had left the party in 1915 to advocate his country's entry into war on the Allied side. Discharged from the army, he had supported the party of those who felt that Italy had been meanly treated in the peace settlement and lent his pen to the advocates of a tough, expansionist policy. (See Chapter VI.)

But a secondary role in nationalist politics did not appeal to Mussolini, and while d'Annunzio strutted in Fiume holding Italy's allies at bay Mussolini found more promising situations to exploit in Italy itself. Inspired by the Russian Revolution, and by an economy bankrupted by war, mismanagement, and the end of Allied aid, a series of strikes were putting the fear of revolution into the Italian propertied classes. The workers were dissatisfied, and they distrusted Mussolini as a renegade. But there were other dissatisfied elements in Italy besides the syndicated workers. Students, soldiers, discharged veterans, unable to readjust to civilian life, disliked the existing order too, although they did not want to replace it with a class dictatorship. It was to these people that Mussolini turned, not to preserve the existing order, but to revolutionize it and, thus, remove those conditions which both justified and favored the revolutionary activities of his "red" rivals.

The first *Fascio di combattimento* was set up in Milan on March 23, 1919. The ideas for which it claimed to stand were far from reactionary. (*See Reading No. 1A.*) The Fascios wanted to dissociate themselves from classical "red" revolution, but their own program was almost as radical: they would put an end to the monarchy; abolished the Senate, the aristocracy, compulsory military service, banks and stock exchanges; confiscate unproductive revenues; attack the money power; decentralize government; protect and educate the poor. Although Mussolini's *Popolo d'Italia* changed its subtitle from "Socialist Daily" to "Producers' Daily," it continued to support the workers revolutionary agitation, and Mussolini himself claimed he had remained a Socialist.

In effect, to begin with, the Fascios supported the strikes that raged throughout North Italy, even the first sit-in strikes of 1919, when the workers took over the factories and challenged army and police to dislodge them. A Fascist resolution of July 1919 affirmed "a boundless solidarity with the insurgent people against those who starve it." In the spring of 1920, the *Popolo d'Italia* criticized the all-engrossing state for its intervention in industrial conflicts on the side of capital against the workers. And when, by August 1920, Mussolini began to look upon sit-in strikes with a critical eye, it was less, he said, because of their threat to the property principle than because of their inefficiency and their lack of perspective. "Had their organizers meant to use them as a jumping board for much vaster ends," he, for his part, would have been ready to accept them. But belly-Socialism, he said, was not for him —nor the limited material ends which alone the unions envisaged. Strikes used for such petty purposes lost sight of the greater aim of a final revolution and could but fritter away the energies and power of the workers. For his part, the Fascist leader envisaged not piecemeal reform, but radical changes. These Mussolini could approve, as he did in a speech delivered at Trieste on September 20, 1920, while a general strike immobilized Piedmont and Lombardy: "I accept not only [*the idea of*] workers' control of factories, but also the social, cooperative, management [*of industry*]. . . . I want industrial production to rise. If the workers could guarantee this rather than the owners, I should be ready to declare that the former have the right to take the latter's place."

In these words we recognize the tone of pragmatic competition which would permit the Fascists to turn from revolution to counter-revolution, from being the rivals of the Communists to being their opponents. One of Mussolini's admirers has called him a *condottiere*—a soldier of fortune—and this provides a clue to the fact that within two years of the radical verbiage of 1919, we find the *fascios* acting as strike-breakers and within three years the professed Socialist Republican being called to power by his king.

It is more than likely that part of the reason for such a switch lies in the Fascists' need for money. But soldiers of fortune seek power even more than money, and Mussolini had realized that in his race for power against the Communists and the Socialists who were firmly entrenched in labor unions and city councils, he could only be successful with the support of the conservative representatives of established order. With the Communists he shared a revolutionary radicalism in which he could never convincingly overbid them; with the conservatives he shared a common Nationalism and a common regard for authority and order, in which the conservatives' inefficiency and their moderation left them at a disadvantage. It was immaterial that for Mussolini the authority and order in question were to be his own; this was a matter to be clarified later. The conservatives could help him attain power. This secured, there was time enough to install an order broadly similar to that which he had advocated in 1919, but adapted rather to the needs of an ever-changing situation than to the points of a particular doctrine.

Mussolini's movement and Mussolini's order, then, appear as the prototype of modern Fascism, which is in effect an opportunistic activism inspired by dissatisfaction with the existing order, but unwilling or unable to proclaim a precise doctrine of its own and emphasizing rather the idea of change, as such, and the seizure of power. Difficult though it may be to conceive, such inspiration can provide a very powerful impetus for a revolutionary movement, the effect of positive statements in politics being generally divisive and that of negative ones unifying. Many a revolution has been carried out by people who did not know what they wanted, but knew very well what they opposed.

Dynamics of Fascism. This was a lesson Fascist leaders never failed to apply: "It would be folly to describe precisely in advance the road by which we shall attain [*our principles*]," writes Oswald Mosley in *The Greater Britain* (1932). "A great man of action once observed: 'No man goes very far who knows exactly where he is going. . . .'" And the Belgian, Léon Degrelle: "You must get going, you must let yourself be swept away by the torrent . . . you must act. The rest comes by itself." Across the border, in France, one of Jacques Doriot's most brilliant followers in the P.P.F. (French Popular Party) sings the same song: "It is not the program that counts; what counts is the mentality of the party that proposes the program," Drieu La Rochelle would write in 1936. "Do not ask us first what is our program, but what is our mentality. The P.P.F. spirit is a spirit of life, of action, of speed. . . ." Doriot was a renegade Communist. His chief competitor, renegade Socialist Marcel Déat, thought the same: "Fervor," he told his followers of the *Rassemblement National Populaire*, "is sometimes better than enlightenment and clarity." (*See Reading No. 1C.*)

What a movement needed to succeed—and it is important to remember that the sense of movement was essential in fact as well as name—was a mystique, a principle, or an idea to which it could appeal, which could sweep its followers off their feet and off their minds, toward a goal left imprecise except in terms of power. "It is not a question of working out a program," a French right-wing terrorist declared: "The question we seek to solve is of a higher order . . . we have to find the Idea, the dynamic of salvation, the dynamic of action. Only an Ideal, only a Mystique, are likely to redeem us, to raise us, to make possible the redeeming ascent towards the bright pinnacles of the future."

The curtain of lyricism discarded, questions do arise, nevertheless: "Ascension towards what?" "Change in what direction?" "Power for what purpose?" and the answers to such questions provide an indication, if not of these movements' doctrines, at least of their tenor.

In this connection, we should do well to remember that Fascism never denied its early social radicalism. On the contrary, it considered itself a form of Socialism, freed of humanitarian sentimentalism and Marxist dialectic, truer to fundamental Socialist aims in that it tried to adapt itself to a changing historical reality which the old Marxist interpretation no longer suited. Socialism, by this time, had become a practically meaningless term. In certain cases, it served as a pejorative label to stick on objectionable men or measures; in others it provided a popular description of desired but undefined reforms. Definitions like "Socialism is equality" or "Socialism is justice" do not go far before they beg the question how this "equality" or this "justice" are themselves envisaged.

Socialist reform has generally been connected with measures carried out following a general plan and involving a redistribution of national income and social influence according to decisions made by specialists in the service of a central power. In other words, as it became effective, Socialism became increasingly technocratic and moved further away from its original moral and humanitarian inspiration. Considerations of humanity and social justice play a smaller part in modern technocratic planning (be it under the impulse of Socialist ideas) than they did in the original Socialism of the 19th century. Material comfort and social and economic opportunity are desired for all, but they are wanted for utilitarian reasons and within the limits of more general interests. The good of the community may not, and often does not, coincide with the immediate good of single individuals. Much of the original inspiration of European Socialism, on the other hand, had come from humanitarian rather than utilitarian concerns. The social romantics of the early 19th century had been moved by charity, not calculation. And it is useful to distinguish between humanitarian Socialists and utilitarian ones. There is little to prevent the latter from operating on the national or indeed, if convenient, the nationalist plane.

Humanitarian Socialism is almost necessarily pacifist and internationalistic, because the same concerns that make men care for their fellows at home apply to human beings everywhere. It is idealistic because it is founded on sentiment and on ideals; being so, it will do best in fairly prosperous societies where a margin for luxury exists. This kind of Socialism is useful as a palliative for the more obvious forms of economic distress and as an educative force, but it tends to collapse before the self-interest of individuals or of the group. Its adherents, then, have the choice between small-scale martyrdom (as in the case of conscientious objectors) and conformity (as in the case of those who suspend their pacifism in wartime).

Utilitarian Socialism, on the other hand, is opportunistic and empirical. It is doctrinaire, but ready to use doctrine in its maneuvers and to adjust its theory to the moment's needs. Its tendency is to consider human beings only as part of groups, in which it sees the significant unit of political calculation. Where humanitarian Socialism is sentimental, utilitarian Socialism tries to be mathematical. And, given this approach, there is no reason to wonder at apparent changes in orientation, such as can be found, for instance, so frequently in Soviet history.

When the Socialism in question is of the utilitarian kind, its combination with Nationalism is possible. Mussolini in Italy, Hitler in Germany, and Perón in Argentina, all claimed that they had revivified Socialism and given it a new efficacy and a fresh connection with historical evolution. Their claims were confirmed by many opponents who, outside of Communist ranks, recognized a characteristic of the Fascist or National Socialist appeal that later observers would ignore: "The National-Socialists, it is essential to remember, call themselves 'Socialist' as well as 'Nationalist,' " wrote the *Daily Herald,* organ of the British Labor Party, on May 2, 1933. "Their 'Socialism' is not the Socialism of the Labor Party, or that of any recognized Socialist Party in other countries. But in many ways, it is a creed that is anathema to the big landowners, the big industrialists and the big financiers. And the Nazi leaders are bound to go forward with the 'Socialist' side of their program." From the opposite pole, a sometime collaborator of Hitler suggests that the speculations of National Communism had not been completely devoid of substance: "The Third Reich," warned Hermann Rauschning, "is actually bringing into operation a sort of socialism. We may call it Prussian Socialism, or State Socialism, or the total mobilization of the nation, or the beginning of the grandiose 'democracy of work.' . . . The revolution will proceed on its course. And it will do so through the initiative of a revolutionary elite in cooperation with masses excited into revolutionism."

While the old order, political and economic, creaked and strained, parliamentary Socialist parties had become part of the establishment, adopting its methods and its ideas of gradual reform which, it was hoped, would reconcile the workers to the common prosperity of the capitalist system. To the left of this conservative Socialism stood the

Communist Party with its slogans of class warfare and its foreign connections. Fascism appeared as an alternative to both, as the representative of a national revolution hostile to conservatism, but opposing social divisions as it opposed social injustice. And when European Socialists gathered in 1934 to study the Fascist question, Henri de Man, leading intellectual of the Belgian Labor Party and soon to become its leader, explained that "Fascism has succeeded because it emphasized the anti-capitalist sentiments to which the Socialist movement no longer appealed enough. Fascism has rallied the masses by a program, by slogans, by a vocabulary that are anti-capitalistic."

Violence and History. The ideological inspiration of this attitude is to be found in the work of such men as Joseph-Arthur de Gobineau (1816-1882) and Friedrich Nietzsche, but also and more immediately in the writings of Georges Sorel. "It is to Sorel that I owe most," declared Mussolini: "For me the essential was to act." The characteristically Fascist form of action, through violence, had been advocated in Sorel's best known book, *Reflexions on Violence,* an attempt to adjust the conventional Marxist analysis of social development to the political and economic facts of 1900. It was naïve, thought Sorel, to put your trust in the gradual proletarization of a society which, contrary to the predictions the *Communist Manifesto* had made in 1848, was becoming increasingly bourgeois and ever less inclined to desperate revolution. On the other hand, those Socialists who, in view of this, hoped to achieve their aims by gradual reforms carried out within the existing system were just as mistaken. The Socialist order could only be installed by a radical revolution; to create the conditions for such a revolution, violence must be used.

Violence is distasteful to sensible men. Worse, history shows it to be a wasteful and ineffective method, likely to corrupt even the worthiest cause. This is because violence has been used in a sporadic or sentimental fashion without calculating the end in view. Violence must cease to be an anarchic reflex. It should be integrated in the order of political action so as to end the dichotomy of two great historical phenomena—order and violence—too often and too wastefully opposed, and to ensure the historical realization of Socialist aims. In this manner, ignoble means were dignified by a noble end, and violence appeared as a morally and socially necessary form of effective action.

Gobineau's *Essay on the Inequality of Human Races* (1853-1855) is also often cited as a basic source of Fascist opposition to the sentimental humanism of an earlier day. This can be misleading for, while Gobineau argues in favor of white supremacy, Mussolini, who had been affected by his ideas, was not a racist. What Mussolini took from Gobineau was not the affirmation of white supremacy, but the idea that power must be based on the collective principle; not on universal human values like honor, freedom, or human dignity, but on biological factors of a collective or social nature: race, nation, or caste. Fascism would justify its aspiration to total control by biological considerations and would define "order" by the coincidence of political and biological realities.

With their insistence on living space and on the survival of the fittest, Fascism and National Socialism appear as the political expressions of evolutionist and so-called Darwinian views. They deny transcendental values because history provides no indication of ultimate truth, and so the only valid approach must be a pragmatic one. It is, indeed, in this attitude that we discern the historical roots of Fascist thought, growing from an intellectual situation in which, following the death of God, history was left as the only touchstone of the absolute—a sort of theology for our time.

The fate and development of nations is the bedrock of Fascist reality. But this reality itself changes, both in time and space. The divine spirit which, according to Hegel, realized itself in the nation's past, could also suggest its future; but this could only be realized by the heroic few who combined the capacity to perceive such a manifest destiny with the courage to carry it out. Courage, here, is very important, for it relates once more to the deliberate activism so characteristic of Fascism. Traditionalists and conservative Nationalists also refer to history in order to justify setting back the clock or staying put. Blood and soil can be considered as a stable reality, as a stabilizing factor, in a situation where least change is best. But when, instead of providing a reference for traditionalists, history becomes the justification of collective, national, or racial evolution and change, when it becomes the only absolute reference of the will to power, then it is the basis of Fascism. The conservative or the traditionalist does not consider history alone and of itself as his sole point of reference. Other references are as authoritative in his eyes: great institutions and organized bodies, guilds, estates, above all the Church. But history, when it becomes the only concrete absolute capable of providing both definition and justification, is no longer referred to (as in Nationalism), in an attempt to be true to it, but envisaged as a continuous creation, as a deliberate acceleration of human destiny entitled to overthrow or crush all obstacles before it.

Once again, this explains why Fascism not only *uses* violence—a trait which is not, after all, peculiar to Fascism —but regards it as an absolute (because necessary) means to an absolute and necessary end. In this perspective, violence appears as the highest or, at any rate, the most obvious form of the social energy and the will to power which *create* history.

Such an analysis may take us further than the theorist of pragmatic Fascism would wish to go. But it applies to the common principles which we can discern among a great variety of Fascisms, all of which imply historical relativism when they argue that history awaits its maker; all of which insist that the nation exists as an absolute, expressing and affirming itself in the role it plays in history, its people incarnated in a heroic leader who embodies the world historical individual of 19th century Hegelian legend.

Given his gigantic task of forging history on the hoof, the leader must be able to call on all the resources of the nation—both spiritual and material. Previous to bending his people's energies to their historical task, he must, therefore, conquer their souls. Writing about the public at one of his meetings, Degrelle expressed this very well: "The crowd was magnificently subdued, entirely given over to an idea, by all its senses, by every fiber of its flesh. But what one sensed above all, and what really made these Rexist meetings worthwhile, was this quality of the soul, this vibration, this total abandon of the public . . . Rex is the realm of total souls, withholding nothing, marching straight ahead, sure of their way. That is the true Rexist miracle: this faith, this unspoilt, burning confidence . . . *We have these souls.* Who could say as much?"

The Leader and the Crowd. The Fascist leader conquers a crowd and subdues it as he would a woman or a horse. But such a conquest implies responsibilities. When a people achieves true national self-consciousness, explains the Romanian, Codreanu, "the leader is no longer a master, a dictator who does what he wants and leads where he wills. He is the expression of that invisible spirit, the symbol of this state of consciousness. He does not do what he wants. He does what he must. And he is led [*by the interests*] of the eternal nation which the people has sensed."

Here is the basis of that cult of the leader as the emanation of his people, produced by his people as the materialization of its profound will and purpose. Such a leader is neither elected nor appointed. He affirms himself as the "truly democratic" chief of a group that freely accepts him. As we have seen, Fascists and National Socialists stress this oneness between the statesman and his people, a people that gives itself to him, trusts him, and loves him. "This is the true popular sovereignty," writes Pierre Daye, leader of the Rexist group in the Belgian Parliament: "leaders who command with authority, but who, by direct contact with their people, feel in constant communion of will and ideas with everything good in the country. When such a sympathy exists, political formulas have little importance." The general will of the nation is now concentrated in one person in whom the people, *his* people, can glimpse their true historical selves, their true destiny, as in a magic mirror in which they see themselves magnified and exalted.

The cult of the leader constitutes an invitation to popular auto-idolatry. Proud of their popular origins and referring to them often, Mussolini, Hitler, Eva Perón, and Degrelle concentrate upon their persons not only power, but emotion, and affection. The identity upon which the leader insists, permits every sparrow to fly vicariously on eagle's wings and to enjoy the eagle's triumphs and his magnificence as if they were his own.

Hence, perhaps, one reason at least for an antiparliamentarism which reflects not only disgust with the old order, but refusal to accept the very idea of delegation and representation. No representative assembly can replace or compete with the leader. When it is not sheer opportunism, therefore, Fascist antiparliamentarism reflects this basic monism, an aspiration to direct democracy.

Totalitarianism. To be complete, the empire of Fascism must extend over minds as well as bodies. From this point of view, Fascism appears as the modern and technologically perfected form of the ancient *polis*—a society totalitarian in its way, all of whose members worshipped the city's god and obeyed the city's rules; and the situation it creates is similar to that which Antigone faced before Creon (where private or transcendental values clash with the ruler's will), or Socrates before an Athenian democracy that could not tolerate mavericks for long. If the community is an organic whole, deviations are corrupting and cannot be tolerated. All must act as one, shunning dissensions as intrinsically harmful, seeking a unity which alone can save in the providential person of one man. As Drieu La Rochelle explained to the followers of Doriot: "Saving France means saving the French, all the French, even those who do not want to be saved, who let themselves go, who ask only to be left alone."

Unity alone can save. The matter is important for, justified or not, Fascism lives and thrives in an atmosphere of crisis. All Fascisms see themselves as a last recourse; all are menaced by a hostile world, in a state of siege where self-sufficiency—material and ideological—is the only hope. Totalitarian autarky thus appears as a further component of the state-of-siege mentality, which in turn is another justification for dramatic violence as the means of history, but sometimes also as its end. "Hope for me is Fascist," the Frenchman Lucien Rebatet would write in *Les Dé-combres* (*The Ruins*) published in 1942; and this hope lies only in a "profound and brutal" revolution, "impossible without violence and radical destructions." Here, the romantic Fascist appears too fascinated by the means to bother much with the end, or to define it further: "One does not compromise with enemies like the Jews, the priests, the committee-mongers, the speculators. One crushes them. One bends them to one's will. . . . Revolutions are not

baptised with holy water, they are baptised in blood. Death
is the only punishment that peoples understand. Death
alone condemns an enemy to oblivion." Such exaltation
over gore and death, such glorification of them, recalls
Mussolini's panegyric of war: "War alone carries all
human energies to the height of tension and leaves the im-
print of nobility on the peoples that dare face it. . . . Perhaps it is a tragic destiny that weighs on man . . . his
fundamental virtues come to light only in bloody struggle."

It is impossible after all this not to speak of romanticism,
the sweet rapture of vague exalting words which inflame the
imagination and stimulate the vocabulary even further.
After the unexpected successes of Rex in the Belgian elections of 1936, the victors signed a sort of manifesto drawn
up by one of the movement's few intellectuals, Jean Denis:
"Rex is not an adventure," the manifesto read in part. "It
is something much more beautiful than an adventure. This
great departure, this moving break with the past, this
fantastic enterprise likely to attract spirits enamored of the
absolute, is an answer to a call that comes from far in the
past, from far in the present." To seek a meaning in what
is evidently an incantation would be a waste of time. It
would be wrong, however, to imagine Fascism limited to
juvenile and demagogic lyricism of this sort or, indeed, to
think that juvenile and lyrical demagogy need be limited
in its effects.

The grandiose displays (both Nazis and Rexists adopted
the color red for their banners), the verbiage and the wind,
were an essential part of great campaigns to conquer souls
and hold them. Power must be attained, national unity
forged, the collective will asserted, by all means. Essentially
democratic, in its propaganda if not in its essence, Fascism
addressed itself to feelings, not to intellect. Rational appeals
are accessible to few; they are also subject to criticism.
Reasoning invites examination, speculation, and disagree-
ment. Feelings can be shared; arguments seldom, and then
by few. Hence, propaganda methods whose essence was
determination and deliberate bias. The Fascist's historical
relativism made academic objectivity seem as impossible
to him as it does to the Marxist. Propaganda, a Rexist
periodical asserted, had to be completely subjective. Ul-

timately, however, the individuality it expressed was that of the nation—the only ultimate to which anything could be validly related.

Elitist Democracy. And, while the national definition implied a kind of equality among all the members of the nation, it also suggested that, as a group, they constituted an elite. Thus, the assertion of the in-group against everybody else—all French being one against all non-French, all Germans one against (and superior to) all non-Germans —provided the groundwork for both equalitarian and elitist argument.

The kind of love relationship between a movement and its people, between a leader and his people, which we have recognized as the basis of a direct democracy amounting almost to a sensual union, also implied equality. Rex always insisted on the identity between the movement and its leaders and the Belgian people. The Romanian Iron Guard was essentially populist, its most devoted followers recruited from among peasants and poor university students. But the most striking instances of this new equalitarianism are to be found in class-conscious Germany, where the Nazi organizations managed to mix the social classes to a degree never achieved before. Comparing the German army of 1940 to that of the Kaiser, Henri de Man was forcibly struck by its social unity, itself an indication of the greater social unity realized in the ranks of the nation itself. The simple ex-Nazis whom Milton Mayer interviewed after the war in a small Bavarian town (*They Thought They Were Free,* Chicago: 1955), cherished the memory of this social revolution: "We simple working-class men stood side by side with learned men in the Labor Front," a baker would tell Mayer. "In the Labor Front," said another, "we belonged to something together, we had something in common. We could know each other in those days. . . ." Even the local schoolteacher, the only one to view Nazism with a critical eye, believed in the reality of democracy as part of its program and practice: "There was democracy in Nazism, and it was real. My—how shall I say it?—my inferiors accepted me."

This crucial acceptance of each other by men of different social classes as equals in the nation, in the party, and in the different party organs whose hierarchy, incidentally, also added to the opportunities of social mixture and promotion, all this supported by incessant equalitarian propaganda and a system whose marks of social distinction differed from traditional ones, had a profound and hopeful effect. Eva Perón's jewelry and stylish dresses were part of her appeal to the *descamisados,* to whom she seemed a symbol of the opportunities that Perón's *justicialismo* was offering to all. Well aware of this, she labored the point: "You will all have clothes like these some day. . . . Some day you will be able to sit next to any rich woman on a basis of complete equality. What we are fighting for is to destroy the inequality between you and the wives of your bosses."

One obvious means for destroying this inequality lay in the party, with its own uniforms which—brown shirts and black shirts, green shirts and blue ones, belts and jackboots —set a man apart from the common run of humanity, proclaimed his membership in a fraternity with values and a hierarchy of its own. The army, too, where the uniform begins by establishing the basic uniformity from which individuals detach themselves by abilities best suited to the army's task, had been an excellent instrument for the abolition of social differences. But the army, which in many countries furnished the last refuge of a haughty and tenacious class spirit, reflected and magnified the privileges and the inequity of societies where money and influence held sway. In any case, most citizens passed through it too rapidly to be marked by its peculiar values.

The war had been different. Between 1914 and 1918, the comradeship and the equality, of the trenches; the opportunities that combat offered for leaders to affirm themselves and men to show their worth without any reference to birth or education—these were remembered fondly by many a combatant. With death and misery past, men recalled the better side. In Germany, Italy, Hungary, and France the first Fascist leagues were founded by men who almost yearned for the chaotic and virile hell that civilians had always ignored, its unity, its order in the midst of chaos, and its opportunities for violent—even if useless— action. The leagues, the movements, and the parties sought to recapture or re-create all this. (*See Reading No. 8A.*) Opposite the Communist Party, with its aggressive class consciousness, the Fascist leagues offered movements as active, where caste was abolished in the comradeship of a new self-styled elite.

Elite is a tricky term. It generally describes a body or group considered to be socially superior. And the elite spirit so prevalent in the movements we know seems at first to contradict their equalitarianism. The meaning becomes clear, however, and the contradiction less, if we remember that the equality which Fascists extolled was one of origin and opportunity, very similar to that which the French Revolution had decreed, an equality from which men detached themselves to the extent that their virtues and their will could carry. Marcel Déat explained this to his followers in some detail in a speech delivered in 1941: The old democracy wanted to persuade the most backward clods that they were equal to the greatest and the best of men. It found no difficulty in doing so but, in the process, envy became a part of a false equalitarianism. Since men were no more equal in democracy than they had ever been, envy became the essence of relations between people who, inevitably, fulfilled different functions in society. But true freedom consists of carrying out your task in the place which suits you and which you deserve, and equality has two complementary aspects: on the one hand, equality of opportunity to begin with—for there can be no difference between men except that of their work, their talent, their true worth; on the other "this higher, deeper, more intimate and indefinable equality which arises between leader and led, from mutual trust and from the absolute certainty that both sides carry out their duties for the common good and solely in order to serve it."

A New Chivalry. To the materialism of a grubby, bourgeois world, the Fascists opposed a doctrine of sacrifice, abnegation, and entire devotion to the cause, similar to that which the good Bolshevik must accept; a doctrine to which they often added the mystical idea of transcendence by expiation. This last was strongest among the deeply Christian Legionaries of Romania for whom "the true and eternal victory [*was*] that born of martyrdom." The same theme recurs on the lips of other nations: "It was by demanding devotion, exalting self-sacrifice, evoking renunciation, purity, labor gladly given, that Degrelle drew the

wildest applause," reports Pierre Daye. Oswald Mosley's
Greater Britain ends with these words: "Those who march
with us will certainly face abuse, misunderstanding, bitter
animosity and possibly the ferocity of struggle and danger.
In return, we can only offer them the deep belief that they
are fighting that a great land may live." But it is Marcel
Déat who reveals the fundamental sentiment most clearly:
"People might ask whether we want to create an Order—
the word does not frighten me. But it has to be understood
as the voluntary acceptance of a strict rule, for the sake of
a great task to which one has resolved to devote himself.
At least, then, the Revolution will have its regulars, as she
will have her secular devotees. And if the future members
of the One Party took the oath of poverty on joining it
. . . it would not be a bad idea. . . . We live in times
when exemplary behavior is essential, especially in those
who want to reform."

Déat's Order might have been one of reforming friars. A
more frequent image is that of the medieval knight. We find
it not only in the Nazi revival of medieval *Ordensburgen*
as training centers for the SS—Teutonic Knights of a later
day—but also in the thought of Eugène Deloncle, who
wanted his collaborationist Social Revolutionary Movement
to be like knights of old. We also find it at Nice in May
1941 when, on the day of the feast of Jeanne d'Arc, Joseph
Darnand, authentic hero of two wars, decided to found a
militia of the Veteran's Legion (*Service d'Ordre Légion-
naire*) which would support Pétain's national revolution,
and to recruit this among young people sharing a common
ideal embodied in the medieval knight. Darnand's S.O.L.
soon became the murderous and bloody militia, feared
auxiliary of the German occupant's Gestapo, but its oath
continued to be administered to trainees on their knees, who
had passed the night in vigil and meditation under arms.

Before a vast public gathered to hear him in Paris on
his return from the Russian front, where the Germans were
already in full retreat, Léon Degrelle, now a colonel com-
manding the Walloon Legion of the SS and speaking under
its auspices, put it all with his usual brio:

> The true elites are formed at the front, a chivalry is cre-
> ated there, young leaders are born. That is where you find
> the true elite of tomorrow . . . and there between us a com-

plete fraternity grows up, for since the war everything has changed. *When we look to our own country and see some fat, stupefied bourgeois, we do not feel this man to be a member of our race; but when we see a young revolutionary, from Germany or elsewhere, we feel that he is one of ours, for we are one with revolution and with youth.*

We are political soldiers, the badge of the SS shows Europe where political and social truth are to be found . . . we prepare the political cadres of the postwar world. Tomorrow, Europe will have elites such as it has never known. An army of young apostles, of young mystics, carried by a faith that nothing can check, will emerge one day from the great seminary of the Front.

There was about these transports a great deal of romance, of histrionics, of enthusiasm for enthusiasm's sake. But the world conceals vast quantities of fervor, great capacities for devotion, that ask no better than to be employed. In a Western world where sometime Radical and Socialist parties had "come to terms with reality," where only Communism still called on an adherent's sense of sacrifice rather than on his search for security or gain, the Fascists offered an alternative, however vain—"a cause" as Degrelle put it, "which transcends the man, asking everything from him, promising nothing."

Nothing for him—of course. But great things for the nation of which he is a part, in which he finds himself the artisan of that unity and self-awareness on which national fulfillment depends.

Organic Society. The assertion of national unity against outside pressure or against internal faction soon brings to mind the image of an organic society in which the free individual, alone in the world, making his own terms with other individuals and with society, is replaced in a complex structure of "realities": his family, his trade, his region, above all his nation, all of which exist prior to him, all of whose existence is essential to his, all of whose security and prosperity are essential to his, to all of which, therefore, he and his private interests must be subordinated.

This, of course, bears heavy marks of Hegelianism. In the 1920's and the early 1930's, we find a leading German advocate of the Corporate State insisting that while private property exists *formally, in reality* there is only collective property. What did he mean by this? Presumably that, while we may think of property as private, and even formally and legally acknowledge it as a fact, the true—Platonic, or Hegelian—reality is that property depends upon and is subject to collective existence, the collective interest, the collective will. This is the principle by which we justify taxation, or the freedom of firemen to trample our lawn when putting out a fire next door, or all the other trespasses we sanction upon property called private.

All so-called right-wing reactions against the liberal democracy of the 19th century have opposed the organic concept to the individualistic one. "Whether Fascism is a philosophy or an intuition, a vision or a faith," wrote Mussolini, "it is always—at least virtually—an organic conception of the world." And because it is organic, however opportunistic its pragmatism may be, the Fascist tendency is towards collectivism. That is why, addressing the French Socialist Party Congress of 1933, Marcel Déat could mention (to the horror of the president, Léon Blum) the possibility that Fascist forms are only a transition on the way to the Socialist society.

It might be, suggested Déat, that one had to go through Fascism "before one could reach a truly Socialist phase of production and distribution." The great Romanian theoretician of corporatism, Mihai Manoilescu, would express a similar hope in his book, *The Century of Corporatism* (1938), welcoming the gradual squeezing out of capital and the diminution of its influence, and expressing the conviction that Italian corporatism would move "willy-nilly" towards "the social Left."

4

SOCIALISM AND NATIONAL SOCIALISM

Fascist Socialism. The extent to which Fascist or National Socialist movements were or were not Socialist or "social" is, we have already seen, a vexed one. The critics of Fascism generally represent it as the vehicle of nationalist ideology in the service of capitalism. A typical statement of this view appears in John Strachey's *The Menace of Fascism,* which the British Labor leader and future minister published in 1933, after abandoning Mosley's New Party. For Strachey, National Socialism is simply a movement "for the preservation by violence, and at all costs, of the private ownership of the means of production. . . . Fascism kills, tortures, and terrorizes in defense of the right of the capitalists to keep the fields, factories and mines of the world as their private property."

Two things strike one in this passage: in the first place, the familiar confusion between Fascism and National Socialism; in the second place, the equally familiar confusion between these movements and reaction. And, since reaction must be defined as the attempt to keep things essentially as they are or, better still, turn the clock back—preferably to a time before the French Revolution—since reaction opposes progressive or subversive tendencies, Blackshirts and storm troopers, Rexists and Romanian Legionaries appear in Strachey's book as simple mercenaries in the service of some occult private interest. This was a mistake that true reactionaries like Charles Maurras never made.

Let us see what another student of Fascism, the Communist theoretician R. Palme Dutt, has to say on this question. In his *Fascism and Social Revolution* (1934) Palme Dutt enumerates what seem to him the outstanding characteristics of Fascism, which may be summed up under seven headings:

1. Maintenance of capitalism;
2. Intensification of capitalist dictatorship;
3. (a) Limitation and repression of independent working-class movements, and (b) building up of a system of organized class cooperation;
4. Revolt against parliamentary democracy;
5. Extending the state monopolist organization of industry and finance;
6. Closer concentration of each imperialist bloc into a single economico-political unit;
7. Increasing imperialist antagonisms, leading to war. (*See also Reading No. 1B*).

On closer examination, we shall find that most of the points which Palme Dutt considered characteristic of Fascism apply equally well to Communism: distrust of parliamentary democracy, extension of state monopolies and state organization, the limitation and repression of independent working-class movements, the concentration of the Soviet bloc into a single economico-political unit, and the exacerbation of imperialist antagonisms both within and outside the Communist world. The maintenance of capitalism and the intensification of the capitalist dictatorship appear ambiguously in the practice of both Fascists and Communists. The latter, at least for the present, operate on the basis of a vast state capitalism whose dictatorship is total or, at any rate, totalitarian; while the former aspire to establish and intensify state control over all capitalist interests of any consequence. There remains the building up of a system of organized class cooperation, which is indeed a fundamental difference between the two systems. And there remains as well a point that Palme Dutt ignored —Nationalism.

One might add in passing that neither Socialism nor Communism is inherently democratic, at least not in terms of constitutional parliamentary regimes based on electoral majorities. A French labor leader and revolutionary Socialist, Victor Griffuelhes (1874-1923), saw the labor movement as "the syndicalist reaction against Democracy." And it is possible to argue that French syndicalism, at least, was born from the proletarian rejection of democratic political processes which they considered heavily weighted against them—as, indeed, they were.

It seems, therefore, that, as concerns fundamental ideology, Fascism differs from Communism—and from Socialism too—by its Nationalism on the political plane and by its insistence upon class cooperation on the social plane. Both of these points have long since been adopted by conventional Socialist, Social-Democratic, and Labor movements in the West, where the essence of Socialism is no longer the victory of one class over another, culminating in the dictatorship of the proletariat, but the reconciliation of the proletariat with their fellow-citizens in an equalitarian (and democratic) national community.

Writing while his country lay under German occupation, Raymond Aron, a supporter of General de Gaulle, forgot all the arguments of Socialist internationalism to remember only the reactions of a romantic Nationalism more redolent of Mazzini than of Marx: The French worker, he declared, knows very well that no social progress is possible in a country enslaved and colonized by a foreign conqueror. Patriotism and the hope of social reform cannot be separated. "These wars of national liberation are true revolutions, because they rouse against the foreign tyrant whole peoples united in the will to fight and to be free." Such arguments would soon be turned against the French themselves by other peoples waging their own revolutionary wars of national liberation against them! But they were also easy to transpose into a National Socialist context, to which Aron acknowledged no relation and no sympathy. If patriotism and the hope of social reform could not be separated, Hitler and Mussolini found an unexpected place in the great Jacobin tradition, along with the heroes of Valmy, the *Communards* of 1871, and the Red Armies that responded in 1918 to Lenin's cry that the Fatherland was in danger as they did in 1941 to Stalin's similar appeal. All this is very confusing, and should warn us to go carefully in trying to find a classification for Fascism. The most obvious conclusion to be drawn from it was voiced by Kurt Schumacher, the German Socialist leader. "Never again," he declared after the Second World War, "will the Socialist be caught being less nationalistic than their opponents."

Some students of Fascism seem to have remained with the conservative view of opposition between extremes, which is reflected in the title of a pamphlet of the thirties: *Bolshevism or Fascism?* The reality lies rather in another title, Drieu La Rochelle's *Fascist Socialism,* which, in an unconventional conjunction, reflects the essence of Fascist radicalism.

If there is one thing all Fascists and National Socialists agreed on, it was their hostility to capitalism. In 1936, the slogan of Rex had been simple:

> Against inhuman hyper-capitalism!
> Against profiteering politicians!
> For bread and dignity!
> Workers of all classes, unite!

Seven years later, Degrelle had not changed his tune: "It is not to save capitalism that we fight in Russia," he told the thousands who had gathered to hear him in German-occupied Paris. "It is for a revolution of our own." Rather than see the old regime survive (or revive), he would prefer the Communists to win:

> If Europe were to become once more the Europe of bankers, of fat corrupt bourgeoisies, slack, sloppy, and accommodating, . . . *we should prefer Communism to win and destroy everything. We would rather have it all blow up than see this rottenness resplendent.*
>
> *Europe fights in Russia because it is Socialist. The youth of Europe which has taken up its machine guns will not make the mistake youth made in 1918. It will not exchange its guns for slippers. We are going to keep our chargers, and when we have put paid to Communist barbarism we shall aim at the plutocrats, for whom we are saving our last shots.* . . .
>
> What interests us most in the war, is the revolution to follow. . . . The war cannot end without the triumph of Socialist revolution, without revolutionary youth stepping in to save the industrial and agricultural worker.

We shall never know whether, had the Nazis won, Degrelle's dream would have come true, the dream of emancipated workers and peasants led by revolutionary youth sporting among the ossuaries and the charnel-houses. The thing to note is that these sentiments were expressed by a

leading National Socialist figure, highly regarded by Hitler
and by Himmler, speaking for the SS who would later
publish and distribute the long speech, with the most revolutionary statements carefully italicized.

Although largely—and often deliberately—ignored, such
tendencies had not (as we have already seen) flared up all
of a sudden. The war may well have given them an opportunity for public expression and a hearing that they
had not always enjoyed. It has generally been argued that
the social pretensions of Fascists and National Socialists
and their revolutionary verbiage were mere camouflage
for sheer opportunistic power politics, designed most often
to preserve intact the essential interests of big money and
big business. In practice, and always remembering that
only in Italy and Germany did such movements achieve
power, and then briefly, the contrary seems to have been
the case. Both Fascists and National Socialists were ready
to compromise, come to terms, moderate their language,
as part of opportunistic political maneuvers. As soon as
they could, however, they tried to establish control over the
economic and financial interests which they had begun by
treating with circumspection.

"Corporatism is not—even in Italy—a system for the
conservation of capitalist privileges," writes Manoilescu.
And in his *Revolution of Nihilism*, written to warn the
West against what he describes as the truly revolutionary
and nihilistic nature of Hitlerism, this is what Hermann
Rauschning says, who had been Nazi Gauleiter of Danzig:
"Nothing is more astonishing than the blindness of Conservative economic and social leaders, not only in Germany but everywhere, to the fact that dynamism, whether
Fascist or National Socialist or any other, is revolutionary,
and that its constructive elements are only in appearance
conservative, and in reality work on the strict lines of
State Socialism, leading of necessity to the expropriation
of the leaders of industry and the deposition of the past
ruling class."

In Italy, the Fascists moved more slowly, first because
the control apparatus of which they had disposed was less
efficient and then because their aims were less doctrinaire
than those of the Nazis. The latter had very little time between their access to power in 1933 and the outbreak of

war, and this time was devoted largely to establishing themselves in power. The liquidation of S.A. leaders in June 1934, which seemed to mark Hitler's break with the radical and Socialist aspect of National Socialism, was only a maneuver in a greater campaign, a temporary sacrifice made to secure long-term advantages. An illuminating article by A. G. Whiteside, "The Nature and Origins of National-Socialism" (*Journal of Central European Affairs,* April 1957), shows that, contrary to Rauschning, some German conservatives at least realized this. Nor did the Nazi rank and file doubt it: as one of Milton Mayer's interlocutors pointed out, to speak of the "National Socialist Party" was to miss the point—it was the National Socialist German Workers' Party. Another had the same to say: "It was the *Arbeiter, Socialist* Party, the Party *of workers controlling the social order;* it was not for intellectuals. . . . People wanted something *radical,* a real change." In January 1939, the *British Union Quarterly* had printed "A letter by an Enthusiastic German National Socialist to a sympathizer in England," protesting against allegations that Hitler was no Socialist. "Hitler is a socialist," the writer insisted: "National Socialism, as the name says, is socialism." If they were not Socialists, it seems at least that this is what they wanted to be.

Property. The confusion between Fascist and Nazi claims of Socialism and the indignant rejection of such claims by a more conventional Left seems to rest largely on the question of property and what should be done with it. Socialists held, and non-Socialists seem to have shared this particular impression, that property was the touchstone of Socialism; and all the theorists of Fascism and National Socialism declared that private property would be respected. They added, however, that property of social significance must conform to the nation's needs and that it would be controlled and directed to this purpose by the state. "All property is legitimate in so far as it does not harm the common interest," Marcel Déat declared. But "as soon as property has a social function it becomes subject to social control." No one is entitled to leave land uncultivated; managers cannot exercise absolute power over their prices, production, or capital; the nation has a sort of suzerain right over private enterprise. In such circumstances, the problem of management becomes more important than that of property—a fact which most economists have realized in our day—and the property regime needs to be modified only to the extent that it is called for by the planned economy of the state.

As a Nazi economist explained in a book published by the German propaganda services in occupied France, the question of private property, which had seemed very relevant a generation before, appeared secondary to National Socialists who approached it with the idea that the general interest is superior to the particular interest. For Nazi economic policy it mattered little whether an enterprise was state-owned or in private hands. The essential was that everyone had to conform to the state's directives. "For an economy thus directed and controlled, the question of private property, apparently essential in 1918, has since become secondary."

Towards an Organized Economy. Thus, corporatist economists could view a mixed economy with equanimity. For Mussolini as for Manoilescu corporatism had no prejudice against either private property or socialization. It was a pragmatic system, which did not set out to impose either one sort of property regime or another. However, it seemed to Manoilescu that, as economic organization progressed, the active economic function of private capital would diminish until, its social utility extinguished, the significance and power of capital would disappear.

This point of view was shared by a Socialist economist like Henri de Man who, in 1934, explained his views to a Socialist study meeting at Pontigny, near Paris. De Man's *Plan du Travail,* which became the official policy of the Belgian Labor Party, envisaged a mixed economy in which "political power would be used to create the economic conditions in which the country's productive and consumption capacities would be adapted to each other. This objective implies a double change in the doctrine of socialization: in the first place, the carrying into effect of a plan on the national plane is no longer subject to the international plane but takes precedence upon it, which means that nationalization must be the present state of socialism; in the second place, the crux of nationalization is not the transfer of property but the transfer of authority

—which means that the problem of management takes precedence upon that of ownership."

Although these views came dangerously close to those expressed by corporatist economists, and which Italy and Germany were beginning to put into practice, the Plan for French Economy elaborated by the C.G.T. (the French Confederation of Labor Unions) and presented by the Confederations leader, Léon Jouhaux (friend and successor of Griffuelhes), followed closely the lines Henri de Man had laid down at Pontigny. (*Compare Reading No. 5A.*)

One wonders how far de Man, steeped in German thought and active in German Social-Democratic circles for many years before Hitler's access to power, had been influenced by ideas of compromise developing in that country, and how far it was on the contrary the thought of de Man which led some German thinkers to emphasize management over ownership. A more general historical explanation, while not answering the question itself, may provide part of the answer. The subordination of ownership to control seems to stem from the attempts of Socialist intellectuals to reconcile their doctrines with a less obviously revolutionary platform, and one which would not clash with property interests that even the working-class electorate now cared for. After the turn of the century, when Socialist parties began to compete for power within the parliamentary system, their collectivistic doctrines could be expressed and applied only at the risk of losing the votes of property owners. As a class-conscious proletarian party, the Socialists could ignore this; as electoral candidates in a democracy they could not—for the industrial proletariat never comprised a majority of the electorate, and small property owners were even more hostile than the great corporations to a collectivism that they interpreted in terms of confiscation and Communism.

For those who proposed a gradual advance towards social justice by means of constitutional reforms, it became necessary, therefore, to adjust Socialist doctrine to the interests and to the prejudices of an electorate for whom property was vitally important. As the Socialists became less revolutionary, their electorate grew and incorporated the partisans of moderate reform within the existing system;

as their electorate grew and their parliamentary representation with it, the Socialist parties themselves became increasingly "governmental"—ready to work with cabinets
of other factions and sometimes even ready to form a
cabinet themselves. This had notably been the case in
France before 1914 and would be the case in Germany,
Austria, Belgium, and Britain in the years which were to
follow the outbreak of war.

It was impossible in these circumstances for Socialists
to emphasize the apocalyptic theses of their Marxist doctrine. It was equally difficult, however, to abandon this
doctrine altogether. The theory had to adjust to practice,
the more so since Socialist theoreticians realized that in an
economic structure, with power increasingly concentrated
in the hands of few, the economy could be manipulated
and directed from a relatively small number of vantage
points that controlled credit, production and labor. Control of capital by a central credit institution which would
regulate interest rates and the flow of money, control labor
through the unions, nationalize key industries (transport,
power), the foundation or acquisition of state enterprise
to serve as guides or checks in other sectors, these would
provide the essential means for vaster changes which need
not threaten, nor appear to threaten, property as such.

The experiments and reforms that all this involved could
only, it seemed clear, be carried out on a national scale.
If the dream of world proletarian revolution was out-of-
date, the hope of a planned economy on a world scale was
as vain. The plan would have to be applied within a closed
society, and one as self-sufficient as possible. Socialism
would have to abandon its internationalism for autarky.

It took some time for such ideas to be accepted. Socialist
militants and leaders continued for the most part to repeat
the conventional slogans of proletarian victory, with their
implications of internationalism, confiscation, and class
war. The first to act along the new lines were the Fascists
and the National Socialists, while corporatist doctrine developed from similar concepts.

It was the great depression, beginning in 1929, that led
Socialists like Mosley and de Man to take a public stand
for protection and national exclusivism. The world economy
based on free exchange had collapsed, effective international

action to cope with the crisis seemed impossible, and so remedial work had to start on the national plane. But even when official Socialist bodies endorsed such views, they found it hard to abandon their hoary class consciousness, and this repelled a portion of the public which might otherwise have gravitated towards them. The economic crisis which turned Socialists inwards towards the nation, had ruined, dislocated, and displaced important sections of the middle and lower-middle classes. Deprived of their property and of their previous social and economic associations, many of these people could now be persuaded to consider collectivistic solutions that they had rejected earlier. Now that they had no property to defend, the thought of a national community of resources became more appealing. They became more willing to express themselves and to view their interests in national-collectivistic terms which seemed to offer the advantage of both utopia and myth: the promise of effectiveness and the inspiration of the dream.

The success of National Socialism in Germany is obviously connected with this. In stressing national unity rather than division into classes, the Nazis harnessed the two great ideological forces of our time. They were not alone. Mosley, Déat, Doriot, and de Man, all insisted that the new society must be a society for everybody, that nothing useful could be built on class divisions; that while the revolution was more than ever necessary, it would not come from petrified party mandarins and bureaucrats trammeled by their investment in the existing order, cracked and useless though this order was.

The Workers. The interest that the new movements showed for the middle classes, and especially for the petty bourgeoisie, has been cited as one more proof of their reactionary nature. We have seen already that Fascist and National Socialist movements can best be described as populist. But they certainly did not lack concern for the worker. When, in 1919, a group of poor and idealistic students at the Romanian university of Iasi founded a movement, which they named National-Christian Socialism, they agreed that defeating Communism (by which especially in the guise of Russian imperialism Romania felt peculiarly threatened) was not enough. "We must fight for the rights of the workers. They have a right to bread and a right to honor. We must fight against oligarchic parties, and set up national workers' organizations which will be able to claim their rights within the limits of the State, not against the State." These Romanian sons or grandsons of shepherds, of farmers, and of village priests were unwittingly close to the Russian *Narodniks,* who had tried to enlighten the peasants, and even to the Bolsheviks whom they bitterly opposed. The first public manifesto that they placed on walls and hoarding of Iasi in the winter of 1919 was headed: "Appeal to Romanian Artisans, Workers, Soldiers and Peasants."

In Hungary, too, the National Socialist Arrow Cross Party led by Major Ferencz Szalasi preached what Szalasi called "a unified socialist community of workers." Very little has been written about these movements of East and Central Europe, and even less of it in English. But according to Professor Istvan Deak's study of the Arrow Cross, a lot of people in Hungary simply thought that the Arrow Cross wanted to introduce Socialism in a form befitting the highly nationalistic preoccupations of a country that was passionately interested in revising the peace terms that were imposed upon it in 1919. Talking about another Hungarian leader of the radical right—General Gyula Gömbös, who was Prime Minister from 1932 until his death in 1936—Deak remarks on the oddity of a situation in which the forces of the "Left" stood for the maintenance of the *status quo,* while the forces of the "Right," mainly under the pressure of the first National Socialists, clamored for social reforms. One might almost say that the Right came to represent the "have-nots," and the Left the "haves."

While the conservatives distrusted the social revisionism and the radical mentality of National Socialism, many workers found it attractive. Workers and artisans accounted for more than half of the membership of Szalasi's party; this proportion appears the more impressive if we consider that only 23% of the economically active Hungarian population was engaged in industry or mining. In other words, workers were heavily overrepresented in the Hungarian National-Socialist movement.

The proportions that we can find in Germany at about the same time are not nearly so impressive, but they still run contrary to the interpretation of Nazism as a reactionary movement. The statistics for 1930 (before the Nazi party came to power) show a little over 28% of the party membership to be industrial workers. The inquiry of an American sociologist (Theodore Abel, *Why Hitler Came Into Power*, New York: 1938), concerning 124 party members who had joined between 1925 and 1927, found 44% of these to have been skilled and unskilled workers, and 7% as coming from Socialist or Communist backgrounds. "At the time of joining," adds Professor Abel, "only 9% were unemployed or in economic difficulties. The rest had secure positions."

It was in 1934 that Abel set out to inquire into the reasons that different Nazis had had (or were prepared to give) for joining the party. He found a significant proportion of working men who liked its promise of a new social order. Many people with social concern, many of whom were workers, had always rejected the doctrine of class struggle or accepted it only superficially. Others found themselves repelled by internationalistic and antinational appeals which placed a vague theory of working-class solidarity above the national and group solidarities they could understand, solidarities which the war had emphasized. Such feelings found expression in the position the National Socialists adopted.

A coal miner was "puzzled by the denial of race and nation implicit in Marxism. Though I was interested in the betterment of the workingman's plight, I rejected [*Marxism*] unconditionally. I often asked myself why socialism had to be tied up with internationalism—why it could not work as well or better in conjunction with nationalism." An old railroad worker said the same thing: "I shuddered at the thought of Germany in the grip of Bolshevism. The slogan 'Workers of the world unite!' made no sense to me. At the same time, however, National Socialism, with its promise of a community of blood, barring all class struggle, attracted me profoundly." And a worker in industry welcomed in the Nazi Party "the uncompromising will to stamp out the class struggle, snobberies of caste and party hatreds. The movement bore the true message of socialism to the German workingman."

As mentioned before, the war had played its part in re-emphasizing a national consciousness which the 19th century had created or inculcated, but which the industrial struggles of the same period had greatly weakened—especially by the turn of the century. By 1918, "United we stand, divided we fall," had acquired more sense than it had had for a long time; and the pragmatic basis for unity had become more apparent in the trenches than it could ever have become from books, or courses in civics. Abel's study quotes many expressions of nostalgia for front-line unity: "The war had taught us one lesson, the great community of the front. All class differences disappeared under its spell. There was only one people, no individuals. Common suffering and a common peril had welded us together."

Even those who were not workers or petty bourgeois were affected by this new sense of what the national community implied and, above all, by the rejection of class distinctions, which were selfish, divisive, corrupting, whoever emphasized them. Thus a great many Nazis expressed their dislike of conservatives, big landowners who cared only for the antediluvian setup in which they thrived, industrialists who were afraid of socialization, and the German National Party—the great conservative party representing all these. They did not like "the spirit of caste and class." One said, "The gentlemen were ready enough to be Germans and Nationalists, but they lacked the courage for socialism." Another Nazi, who had been an active member and organizer of the National Party, left it for the same reason, finding that it did not care about the millions of unemployed but only about the economic interests of its overstuffed members.

A sometime-militant of the subversive youth movement called the Werewolves was sickened by the class prejudice of conservative circles. Germany and the German people could only be revivified through the union of *all* the Germans; but the conservative nationalists did not seem to care: "Reactionary circles were well aware that we were fighting for a nationalistic Germany; still, they continually excluded working men from the national community." So, he turned against them. And a Free Corps volunteer, who had fought the Bolsheviks in the East, very soon realized upon returning home that he and his friends had little in common with the so-called nationalists who "spoke of Germany, but meant money and privilege." He discovered an obscure party that called itself the German Social Party: "It was German, of course . . . German, patriotic, nationalistic . . . that was what we were, and so were the gentlemen with whom we could not agree. But there was another word that aroused our enthusiasm . . . *Socialism*, enlightenment, the development of the communal spirit. . . . We sensed and we knew that if we succeeded in animating these printed words, if we could unite the concepts of nationalism and socialism, we would have a banner under which we could lead the German people to freedom."

In Romania, Codreanu and his friends had much the same impression. No one, wrote Codreanu, not even a worker or a peasant, had the right to pursue his "right" or his "due" at the expense of national unity. "But we also refuse to admit that in the shelter of tricolor formulas an oligarchical and tyrannous class should install itself on the backs of the workers and literally skin them alive, whilst it intones endless appeals to the Fatherland it does not love, to God in whom it does not believe, to the Church where it never sets foot, to the Army which it sends into war with empty hands. *There* are realities which cannot serve as emblems for political swindles in the hands of immoral political conjurers." (*See Reading No. 4A.*)

Romania and Hungary did not have a very politically-conscious electorate. But Germany did. An important proportion of this public was made up of nationalists whose social concern prevented them from accepting the privileges of the conservatives and of collectivists whose national sentiments opposed them to Marxist internationalism. These two powerful currents existed before Hitler and were independent of his movement. As the Free Corps volunteer told Abel—why not unite Nationalism and Socialism? As the coal miner said, why should not Socialism work better in conjunction with Nationalism? Patriotic feelings demanded and commanded national unity; ideas of social justice found exploitation, economic inequalities, the caste spirit reprehensible; wartime experience suggested a very concrete kind of brotherhood, which had seldom been realized before.

Manoilescu was to write that "social service is the source of every right," and that a man deserved a political importance proportionate to his social, cultural or economic

function, that is, to his *national* function. At a simpler
level, many Fascists and National Socialists would agree
with the Nazi factory worker who had been a Socialist because, he said, "it seemed to me no more than proper that
anyone who had unstintingly devoted himself to the Fatherland should be entitled to share its wealth." The man
who expressed these feelings was going back, unbeknownst
to himself, to the very sources of organic nationalist doctrine in the thinking of French and German revolutionaries
of the late 18th and early 19th centuries. From these
feelings it would appear that neither the petty bourgeois
nor the working-class supporters of National Socialism
thought of it as a movement of reaction.

Reformism or Reaction. The equation between petty
bourgeoisie and reaction raises a more serious question,
however, by the implication that an exclusive identification
with the industrial working class distinguishes the party of
progress. It is possible to argue in purely Marxist terms
that in underdeveloped societies, such as Hungary and
Romania, the petty bourgeoisie was a temporary representative of progress. Leaving this aside, the fact remains
that in most countries economic and social progress has
tended to turn the sometime-proletarian into a small
property owner. While many small producers and businessmen are eliminated by modern economic developments,
others find in them the reason of their being. And the
factory worker with a house, garden, and car—or the possibility of acquiring them—is as much of a petty bourgeois
as Mr. Kipps.

In such circumstances, accepted political classifications
like Right and Left lose their meaning. Most people between
the wars would have agreed with George Valois that
basically the Right was static and the Left dynamic; but,
Communism apart, no movement of the time could match
the dynamism of Fascist leagues. In 1931, Jacques Kayser,
a leading figure of the French Radical-Socialist Party, defined the typical left-winger as a man who seeks solutions of
an internationalist nature, defends collective rights against
particular interests, does not consider that present needs
can be answered by the *status quo,* and does not regard
the existing property system as the legitimate foundation
of social order. All but the first of these traits apply per-

fectly to the Fascist militant and, within two or three years, the "Left" too had abandoned its internationalism. Kayser equated the Left with evolution, protest, and movement. There was little there that a revolutionary of the Right would not claim for himself. And just because the classic representatives of such reputedly left-wing values failed to act upon their professed beliefs and failed to adapt them to the moment's needs, the Fascists found a public to attract—the very public that Socialism had lost.

The petty bourgeoisie of labor, the declining middle classes, the rural smallholders, the agricultural laborers, were all largely ignored by conventional parties and doctrines. Neither liberalism nor conservatism, neither social-democracy nor traditionalist reaction, responded to the issues and the needs of these sections of the public. It was to answer these needs—or to speculate upon them—that many Fascist leaders first broke away—Mosley from Labor, Degrelle from the Belgian Catholic movement, Déat from Socialism, Doriot from Communism.

Over a score of deputies left the French Socialist Party (S.F.I.O.: French Section of the Workers' International) in 1933, arguing that social-democracy no longer suited an age where strong and independent executive power alone, based on a reconciled, united, disciplined nation, could tackle the moral and economic crisis. This had also been the gist of Mosley's case in the *Manifesto* he had published on December 8, 1930. And on May 21, 1934, speaking to the Congress of the new *Parti Socialiste de France,* Marcel Déat would argue that the word "nation" now carried more revolutionary overtones than any old-fashioned class slogan. This was especially true when it was used, as the Germans used it, in terms like *Volksgemeinschaft,* meaning "the community of the united nation," envisaged as a classless and socially integrated state where surviving social and economic inequalities would gradually disappear in a new order.

In this new order, the role of the state would be crucial, not only as the representative of the national will, but also as the vehicle of revolution. "It is no longer by revolution that one can attain power," Henri de Man told an audience at the Sorbonne, "it is by power that we can realize the revolution." For this, a strong state was necessary; Socialists realized this as well as Fascists. De Man's "Theses of Pontigny" (September 1934) were inspired by authoritarian and corporatist principles that opposed the traditional concepts of social-democracy. They called for a break with the doctrine of the separation of powers "dear to the heart of bourgeois democracy," and for a regime where "the Executive governs and representative institutions control." In an organic society, the separation of powers makes no sense; but when the Executive governs, in the total sense in which de Man used the term, there is little that representative institutions can do to assert their control. In Germany and Italy, in Vichy France and, later, in the Fifth Republic, just as under Napoleon's rule, representative bodies would serve a symbolic and decorative function, not an organic one.

But if the state is all, and the "representative" bodies politically insignificant, private interests are hardly more effective. Property remains free in direct relation to its social insignificance, but it is manipulated as soon as its existence becomes relevant to public policy. This means that large-scale industrial and money interests will be the first affected. In Fascist Italy and in Nazi Germany, although property was not attacked, its freedom of action was nibbled away, its independence gradually restricted, and its status altered. On August 5, 1932, Mosley's *Blackshirt* quoted Mussolini with approval: "Under Fascism the capitalists will do what they are told and will go on doing what they are told until the end."

By their control of labor, credit, and taxation, Fascists and Nazis tightened their grip on their countries' economies. True, the directors of state boards of control were often chosen from the ranks of industrial and financial leaders. But while these leaders may have acted as representatives of their class and caste, they represented above all the technocracy, the managerial class, whose rise has been a characteristic of our time. Whether their positions are in the public or private sector, these managers seem to act above all as specialists whose personal interests are tied less to ideas of profit and loss than to criteria of achievement in which immediate gain may be irrelevant. Men like these can pass without difficulty from the private to the public sector, distinguish themselves by liquidating a factory or a coal-mining area as easily as by augmenting its productivity, and pass on to the next assignment. We see them at work today in the mixed economy of the United States or the Common Market, as in the state capitalist economy of the Soviet bloc. They are the creatures of the great industrial concentrations of our time, but hardly their servants.

Here again, the national collectivism of Fascists and National Socialists inclines them to view old-fashioned industrial and capitalistic interests with suspicion. Their feeling of being besieged, their insistence on national self-sufficiency, while they may bring profits to national industry go counter to the cosmopolitan tendencies of large-scale money powers. Against anarchic, individualistic or monopolistic capitalism, the theoreticians of Nationalism and of Marxism, the prejudices of proletarians, petty bourgeois and conservatives, coalesce. Their widely divergent interests are reconciled in opposition on the basis of a common Nationalism. The fact that for some this Nationalism is conservative and for others collectivistic is generally and conveniently ignored, so long as the coalition lasts. But such coalitions do not last long.

Temporary alliances between radicals, conservatives, and reactionaries can hold together only under extremely critical conditions—during a time of crisis. The crisis passed, the fever abated, such alliances are bound to fall apart, with the consequent sacrifice of the weaker partners. In Spain and in Romania, the revolutionaries of the Right were neutralized by their conservative competitors; in Germany and Italy, as Fascists and National Socialists settled into power, the conservatives were edged back and gradually removed from positions where they might have exercised an influence on policy or on the economy.

Results were unpleasant in either case. In Spain the representatives of established order did not hesitate to use the Fascist bands to do their dirty work. Mercenaries of a bourgeois order which they detested and which detested them, the Fascists felt exasperation mount at the thought that they were preserving not only the interests but also the good conscience of the conservatives. Where the forces of conservatism moved in time, as Franco did in Spain, this exasperation did not have time to explode: the

Falange was broken and harnessed to the conservative dictator's orders. Failing that, an explosion—such as occurred in Romania in 1941—might lead to massacres ending in defeat and dissolution for the revolutionary insurrectionists.

In the opposite case, however, where the forces of Fascism gained the upper hand, their revolutionary pretensions gave way to opportunistic maneuvers, and high purpose yielded to corruption and parasitism defended by terror and force. The elevation of the end had justified the basest means; in turn, the means would mark the end. The violence glorified as a necessary part of national revivification would sink to brutality. Organicist dogma would justify the constraint or elimination of dissenters. The leader cult ended in paranoiac exclusivism. And the chivalry of the elite turned into a corps of torturers and butchers. Strange paradox of dreams that turned into nightmare, the Fascist phenomenon leaves us with the question, as yet unresolved—at what point and under just what pressures do high ideals turn into tales of dread?

— 5 —

A RED HERRING: RACIALISM

The Nation and the Alien. If National Socialism is so very social, if corporatism leads to state control, and if the National Socialist ideal is a sort of state Socialism (as Rauschning claimed), then what is there to set them apart from Communism—at least in implication, if not in basic theory?

Ideologically speaking, one difference overshadows all the others: for Marxists, the fundamental historical expression of material reality is the class; for Nationalists—as the name implies—it is the nation. To stress class divisions, as reactionary snobs do; or class warfare, as Marxists do, is the supreme betrayal of the unity essential to the welfare and the *existence* of the nation.

Here it might seem appropriate to consider the Jewish question. Aside from the sheer demagogic advantage of appeals based on age-old prejudices which are often of religious origin, anti-Semitism can be traced to three different grounds: the first and the most obvious is part of a purely national argument that may be found in Codreanu's *Credo* of February 1920, which begins: "I believe in one united Romanian State . . . including all Romanians and only Romanians." It can also be read in the twenty-five points of the German Workers' Party, published in February 1920, exactly sixteen days after Codreanu's *Credo,* where we find the assertion that "none but the members of the nation may be citizens of the State. None but those of German blood . . . may be members of the nation. Anyone who is not a citizen . . . may live in Germany only as a guest." (*See Reading No. 2A.*) The citizen of ancient Athens or Corinth would have recognized such concepts, and he would have found familiar Marcel Déat's (rather reluctant) explanation of his Jewish policy: "The Jew is a foreigner—treat him like one. If he is useful to society, he may live on our soil. If he has served in the army, fought for our country, he is accepted as an honorable and honored ally. If he is harmful, let him be expelled." (*See Reading No. 8 B.*)

Theoretically—or potentially—in a state of siege, the nation can afford to tolerate foreign elements (whether these be Hungarians in Romania, Protestants in France, Germans in Poland . . .) only on the most temporary or strictly utilitarian basis. And the obvious foreigner everywhere, partly because he is forced to be one, partly also by self-definition, is the Jew. Thus, on principle, if no aliens, then no Jews.

So much for the theoretical argument. The economic argument is largely pragmatic, and it appears especially in places where Jews traditionally or temporarily fulfilled a certain economic function.

In Hungary, Jews numbered about 6% of the population, yet 49.2% of the lawyers, 24.4% of the doctors, 31.7% of the journalists were Jews, and 46% of all industrial enterprises were owned by persons of the Jewish religion. In Romania, over 11,000 of the 14,300 bank and commercial employees in the capital were said to be Jews; the stock exchange consisted of 139 Jewish and only 3 Romanian brokers; the Bucharest bar included 3475 Romanians and 1390 Jews, while in the country as a whole almost a third of the lawyers belonged to a community whose membership was about 1/25 of the total population. The proportions were similarly striking in Austria.

Even when they are correct, such figures mean little in themselves and justify nothing. Misleading statements, we have been told, are of three kinds: lies, damned lies, and statistics. But they need be no less effective for all that. Justified or not, figures of this sort reflected and seemingly confirmed widespread prejudices which anti-Semites did not fail to exploit.

All over Eastern and Central Europe a good part of big industry, consisting of many of the great department stores and important sections of banking and credit, were in Jewish hands. Small shopkeepers in the provinces were often Jewish too, for example, 117 out of 120 druggists in Bessarabia. The poor native gentry going into business and industry, the rising local petty bourgeoisie just emerged from the land, the newly developing native professional classes were all finding the Jews in their way. The anti-Semitism of the conservative upper classes seldom went beyond the limits of social snobbery and social exclusion. But the radical right's appeal to the middle and lower-middle classes was strongly based on anti-Semitic resentments. The conservatives needed and got Jewish capital and credit for their enterprises and estates, Jewish loans for their speculations; they had no intention of upsetting existing property arrangements in order to confiscate Jewish property. There was no knowing the effect of such gestures. The radical right, on the other hand, were as ready to get rid of Jews as the Communists were to get rid of capitalists, and for the same reason: the radical right saw the Jews as barring the way, materially dominant, and restricting their possibilities of advancement by their very existence. They may well have resented the ability of a more studious, skilled and industrious group, whose separateness seemed flagrant and whose success they liked to attribute to the peculiar solidarity they themselves seemed to lack.

This one-sided appreciation of the situation had the same partial truth as the hungry feeling entertained by colonial nationalists who think that when their occupiers are thrown out there will be more places for them. And this feeling itself is connected with a sense of difference between colonials and natives, as between Jews and Gentiles.

In connection with this feeling of difference, so important to nationalists as to all adherents of an in-group creed, the Jews served a particular purpose which deserves to be mentioned.

Fascists and National Socialists attacked all divisive and corrupting elements, but they had to believe or pretend that their fellow nationals, even if they were superficially corrupted were by their very nature fundamentally sound. This was where the Jew's traditional role of scapegoat acquired a particular importance. A petty tradesman who joined the Nazis during the depression explained to Professor Abel: "In 1926 I had to give up the shop and see my stock and goods sold for a pittance because of my creditors' Jewish partners." An unskilled laborer referred to "the artificial whip of scarcity wielded by the Jews, which sent workingmen scurrying from their homes to beg for food from farmers. . . ." The shopkeeper's Aryan creditors were all right: *they* would not have foreclosed if their Jewish partners had not forced them to. It was also the Jews who wielded the whip of scarcity. There is, quite naturally, no mention of the complex market or policy decisions responsible for the workers' misery; but there is no criticism either of the farmers who hoarded food, and squeezed the city for all they could get.

In the same way, Codreanu pointed out that the leaders of the Communist Party in Romania were Jews and, after listing their names, added: "around them a number of wayward Romanian workers." (*See Reading No. 4B.*) The poor Romanians had been led astray, and French Nationalists like Maurras would sing a similar tune. If only the evil alien influences were removed the natives would return to the national fold. The psychological trick is clear, but it is being played on the nationalist as well as on his au-

dience. Most of these people are sincere. That they are
fooling themselves is another matter: sincerity has no
intrinsic value. A sincere fool is still a fool, a sincere in-
quisitor is still a torturer, a sincere anti-Semite may be any
number of things: in this particular connection he often
appears as a would-be social revolutionary led astray by
too facile and too narrow identifications.

A Convenient Diversion. The way in which anti-
Semitism has served as a diversion for social resentments
appears quite clearly in the work of Edouard Drumont,
the leading publicist of French 19th-century anti-Semitism,
whose politics were "social" and anticapitalistic. If Drumont's great success of 1886, *La France juive,* was a reactionary book, the reaction it expressed was against the
money power, against what the Duc d'Orléans, pretender
to the French throne, called "anonymous and vagabond
wealth" and the corrupting effects of such wealth upon
society and the state. His point of view was close to that of
contemporary Socialists, who also equated moral and political action, and to whom anti-Semitism seemed natural at
a time when Jew was synonymous with usurer or banker,
and the Rothschilds and Péreires were symbols of high
finance.

The Socialists, however, moved past such primitive equa-
tions, while Drumont's approach to the social question
remained naïvely simple. His nationalistic enthusiasms fed
on firm belief in a plot theory of history that saw everywhere the ill-concealed hand of Judeo-Masonic treachery
in the service of corrupt and corrupting capitalism, while
his social concerns were exasperated by hatred of the
capitalist enemy whose interests demanded the perdition of
the proletariat and the ruin of France.

Today, anti-Semitism is no longer the absolutely necessary concomitant of national or socialist attitudes. But old
habits die hard, so do old prejudices, and the Jew reappears
as the symbol of the rootless and possibly subversive alien
where, before, he had stood for the occult money power.
Nationalists and Socialists would do better to realize the
irrelevance of the Jewish question to their concerns. Yet
if anti-Semitism is irrelevant to the basic concerns of
Nationalists and Socialists, it is hardly irrelevant to their
failure. It appears, above all, as the classic red herring

which—with the suggestion of obscure malevolent intrigues on the part of powerful and hidden plotters—can turn from its course a social analysis that threatens to pierce through the nonsense curtain of press and pretense. Once we begin to understand the significance of anti-Semitism as an aberration, we can understand the fate of National Socialism much better. The prophets and the tenets of National Socialism needed money to become effective on the public plane, and they obtained this money from men whose interest it was that they should not become effective. The enemies of anonymous and vagabond fortunes were encouraged to pursue their quarry in directions as insignificant as they were superficially exciting. *The Protocols of the Elders of Zion,* a 19-century forgery purporting to show the Jewish conspiracy to seize world power, furnished the prototype of such conspiracies. The Jews with their supposed racial community, formed the core of a vast international underground that also included Masons hidden behind mysterious rites and certain maverick financiers.

Thus, men who started out with the excellent idea of tracing and neutralizing the doings of diversified and irresponsible money powers that weigh upon their nation and the world were quite literally led astray: taken over, or persuaded to campaign on side issues which combined glamor for the public and innocuousness for the interests they might have threatened. And every would-be-Socialist league found its national-minded backers eager to support campaigns that would combine the excitement dear to activist hearts with the inefficacy demanded by the money interests they represented. Heavy industry—mining and transport, champagne and perfumes—provided the funds for Fascist and National Socialist leagues in Germany, in Italy, and in France. Money, in countless millions, from business, oil, textiles, sugar, alcohol, gas, electricity, and other sources flowed into the coffers of newspapers and parties ranging from extreme right to almost extreme left, with only one end in view: the domestication of men and political movements, which, whatever their professed opinions, could in the end be used for the concrete ends of invisible and irresponsible money interests.

The Communist resistance leader Gabriel Péri attributed this deliberate purpose to the Nazis: "Nazi leaders," he

had written in a tract published in 1942 after his capture
and execution by the Germans, "turned popular anti-capitalism into a rough and barbarous anti-Semitism. Jew was
identified with banker, 5-and-10 cent store owner, Anglo-
Saxon creditor. There as everywhere, anti-Semitism has
been the cunning way of turning away popular anger from
the struggle against the regime of oligarchical exploitation." But even a heretical Socialist like Marcel Déat
sensed that anti-Semitism was a dangerous deviation, that
once one had brayed its slogans, the revolution was still
no nearer. "Personally," Déat told a meeting of his R.N.P.
in German-occupied Paris, "I fear that many of the most
virulent anti-Semites have only one thing in mind, and
this is to divert attention from the essential things that
remain to be done, so that the revolution will be forgotten."
The anti-Semitic and anti-Masonic campaigns of many
radicals of the Right are a good example of how inability
and unwillingness to get to the bottom of things can be
disguised into a semblance of forceful and effective action,
convenient for all parties except the persecuted.

The heritage of Drumont has remained to confuse the
issues and to subordinate efficacy to morality which is no
more than pseudo-morality, in the manner of an earlier
age. It offers a vast treasure-trove of simple and fascinating
explanations, as full of obscene enemies and fair maidens
as a Gothick romance and about as factually accurate.
The Jews, the Masons, the various enemies of the people
are still presented as facile but convincing explanations for
difficulties which have other, and otherwise perceptible,
causes. These rationalizations excite, they mislead, they
sentence to failure, perfectly well-meaning people who
made the mistake of beginning their social studies in the
works of men like Drumont.

The worst of this is that the plot-theory of history
carries with it a hint of the truth. Things do go on behind
the scenes, within the old-boy network, which historians
hardly ever manage to approach. But where Drumont is
terribly mistaken and misleading is when he assumes a
peculiarly effective fraternity among Masons or Jews (or,
for that matter, Protestants) and, hence, a group significance that is not there. The arguments which he bases upon
this assumption are rather like the practice of the popular

press, whose intimate insipidities concerning stars, queens, and babies direct attention upon what is irrelevant and inessential and, by their emphasis of private and passional factors, discourage or deflate all accurate analysis of public affairs. Instead of serving up the secrets of some princely alcove, Drumont pretends to offer those of politicians and financiers. This is supposed to be "reality": the revelations and true confessions of a mysterious conspiratorial realm. His readers, conditioned to consider group solidarities natural (racial, national, class solidarities that they know and understand), accept the analyses he offers and, with them, many of his other ideas. The analysis is mistaken whenever it seeks to generalize on the basis of isolated facts; the ideas are out of date, and the Drumont tradition can only lead to error. This has been the fate of nationalists who have operated within it—that is of most National Socialists with the exception of Marcel Déat, whose theory has always been better than his practice.

Oddly enough, one of Hitler's greatest enemies would claim that Nazi racialism served exactly the opposite purpose, that the reality of Nazism behind its confusing make-believe was "the revolutionary extremism revealed not in its philosophy but in its tactics." But Rauschning's division between racialism and extremism seems unwarranted. Events have shown that for the Nazis the racial delusion was an obsession to which they clung to the last.

But while such myths are not a necessary part of National Socialism, let alone of highly pragmatic Fascism, we can recognize in them a *means*—a justification for propaganda and terror, a biological reference for the definition of a "necessary," "natural" national unanimity. (*See Reading No. 2B.*) From this point of view, racialism appears as an attempt to provide a concrete, would-be scientific basis for national unity. Cultural and linguistic differences are obvious, physical differences are more obvious and hence still more useful, facilitating the assertion that one color or skull formation (my own) is superior to another. The demagogic appeal of racialism is too evident for it to be abandoned by the national-populists of our time; but it would be wrong to connect it automatically with the doctrines discussed in this book.

ITALY

Roots of Revolution. There was no good reason for Italy to enter the First World War; there were many reasons why she should not: the conquest of Libya (1911 and on) had exhausted her army and her resources, Socialists and Anarchists were numerous and active, industry was weak, the country was overpopulated, underdeveloped, and not very thoroughly united under the rule of the house of Savoy. Italians still lived under Austrian government in the Alto Adige and the Trentino, and Nationalists did not cease to call for reunion of the unredeemed provinces to a fatherland that had only been put together half a century before; but the Triple Alliance which bound Italy to Austria and Germany had been renewed as recently as 1912, and Austria was prepared to be conciliatory to safeguard her southern borders. From the Central Powers, Italy could expect important concessions as the price of neutrality; she chose to accept more grandiose assurances as the price of her intervention. In April 1915, by the Treaty of London, the Allies promised her Trentino and the Alto Adige, Istria with the port of Fiume, and Dalmatia: the Adriatic would once more become an Italian sea. In May, Italy was at war, with a cabinet of national union that included the heretofore pacifist Socialists.

For a country ill-prepared and ill-equipped for modern warfare, the conflict was difficult and harsh; the army, on the verge of disaster in 1917, was saved from collapse only by prompt Allied intervention with troops, credits, and supplies. The peace in many ways proved worse: refusing to accept the provisions of the Treaty of London, which the United States had not signed, President Wilson supported the Adriatic claims of the new Yugoslav monarchy. Italy made important gains, but not all the gains for which she had bled. Dalmatia remained in Yugoslav hands, the port of Fiume was left to an international commission: to those who weighed benefits in the balance against corpses, this seemed too little for 750,000 dead and a million wounded.

The morrow of victory was full of disillusion, uncertainty, and confusion. While demobilization and the closing of war factories threw thousands of unemployed into the streets, wartime inflation, which had not ended with the fighting, continued to soar. There were strikes; there was violence and bloodshed; the petty bourgeoisie and the veterans echoed the nationalist complaints about the Allies' treatment of their country. The worn formulas to which old parties clung held no more meaning for the new mass public, prewar Socialist leadership was discredited by its acceptance of the war, and the Socialist Party, joining the Communist international, drifted ever closer to Communist positions. Peasants were taking over the great estates; sit-in strikes and riots threw industry and the cities into confusion. In September 1919, Gabriele d'Annunzio (1863-1938), well known as a poet and as a daring flyer during the war, took the law into his own hands and occupied disputed Fiume with a hodgepodge force of volunteers and regular soldiers. Ensconced in his Istrian fief, he laid plans for a march on Rome and for a new corporatist constitution. He addressed his followers from palace balconies and led them in chorused warcries and slogans with which the world later became familiar. Around him storm troops, the *arditi,* gathered; slogans were hammered out— "A chi e Italia?" "A noi!"; the mood developed which Mussolini would eventually exploit.

Mussolini. Starting as a schoolteacher, Benito Mussolini (1889-1945), son of a Socialist country blacksmith, had fled to Switzerland to avoid conscription and then returned under an amnesty to do his military service. In the years before the war he had become the leader of the extreme wing of the Socialist Party and editor of the party newspaper in Milan, *Avanti!* His pacifist and antimilitaristic intransigence changed very suddenly in November 1914 to violent interventionism which, forced to leave *Avanti!,* he would express in a paper of his own, the *Popolo d'Italia,* probably financed by Franco-British funds. Forsaking Marx, he placed the *Popolo* under the patronage of Napoleon and Auguste Blanqui, the 19th-century Socialist, who had conceived revolutionary action as the preparation of a decisive coup to seize power and establish the workers' dictatorship.

After a year on the Austrian front, Mussolini was invalided home and henceforth free to devote himself to politics and to the *Popolo d'Italia*. For a man who combined an anarchistic kind of Socialism with extreme nationalist positions, the postwar situation afforded Mussolini excellent opportunities for fishing in troubled waters. Mussolini always claimed that he remained a Socialist: as late as 1941, he would affirm it to Marshal Antonescu of Romania, as he would again in the program of the rump "Socialist Republic" which he ruled by German fiat from 1944 to 1945. But the debates, before the war and after, which tore Italian Socialism apart had shown, if nothing else, that there were many interpretations of Socialism. The Socialist Party, though it was winning votes, seemed to have lost the revolutionary spirit; the Communists, on the other hand, took orders from abroad. Another revolutionary party was needed. Blanqui had been the first Socialist to envisage the revolutionary as a professional. He suggested that the success of revolutionary parties must be organized along military lines. Against the organization of the Bolsheviks, only a similar organization could compete: on March 23, 1919, the *Fasci di combattimento* with an extremely radical program which did not at first evoke much public interest, was organized. D'Annunzio was in the limelight, and Mussolini supported him; but the electors who knew d'Annunzio did not know Mussolini. Less than 5000 Milanese voted for the Fascists in the elections of 1919.

Soon, however, d'Annunzio let himself be dislodged from Fiume and from fame. Meanwhile, faced with growing social disorder, the government had decided to use the *fascios*—declared enemies of the "reds," but the only ones "popular" and tough enough to face them—to crush the strength of popular demands, of the Slovenian peasant movement in the countryside around Trieste, of strikes, of squatters, of Socialist and Communist municipal councils in towns and in the countryside. Armed by the army, protected by the police, subsidized by the landlords, the industrialists, and by the government itself, the *fascios* grew in numbers and in force: the movement which had had 35 branches in 1919, had over 800 branches by 1921—over 100,000 members. The *fascios* so effectively raided, burned, murdered, and terrorized in the defense of order that Mussolini and 35 other Fascists, "anti-parliamentary, anti-democratic, anti-Socialist, anti-Government," entered Parliament in the elections of 1921. Within a few days the government had fallen; within a few weeks (November 7, 1921) the Fascist Party was founded and boasted 320,000 members; within a few months governmental instability (for which the Fascists were responsible) inclined many of the respectable, conservative public to welcome the possibility of dictatorship.

At first, the dictator envisaged had been d'Annunzio, but he was disinterested or unwilling to make the necessary efforts. Mussolini was both interested and willing, and a number of politicians, unaware of just what he had in mind, viewed with equanimity the coming of a Mussolini government. This would confront the Fascists with the responsibilities of power and, in due course, saddle them with the same failures and discredit as everybody else had experienced. Thus, when Mussolini revived d'Annunzio's old idea of a march on Rome, he found all resistance melting before him. The unions, still sufficiently active to frighten, were too weak for effective opposition; the officer corps was sympathetic; the government was unusually incompetent even for that day; the king was inert; the opposition was flabby. With the connivance of a palace *camarilla,* the "march on Rome" which would have ended in disaster had the army received orders to oppose it, became a Blackshirt triumph, and Mussolini became premier of the land (October 27-31, 1922).

A Corporatist State? The next few years would be devoted to concentrating power in his hands, eliminating or bringing to heel all possible critics or opponents, and establishing the rule of the Fascist Party (purged of its unreliable elements) in all parts of the country and its life. The press, the courts, the youth, the unions were all firmly controlled; the legislative power reduced to a minimum was going to be replaced by a Corporative Chamber; the Church abandoned its hostility for a concordat with a regime in which it saw a rampart against the reds.

And it is true that big industry, big landowners, and big banks, too, had reason to appreciate how Socialist and syndicalist institutions were destroyed, how strikes and lockouts were effectively forbidden, and how disciplined the mass of workers had become. But if the Fascist unions could control the workers, they could also negotiate from strength with the employers. The more solidly Fascism established itself in power, the more its grip on the country's industrial and credit system tightened. Beyond the parasitism and the corruption, beyond the proliferating Fascist bureaucracy, there loomed the social doctrines of the Corporate State so well reflected in the beginning of the Labor Charter of 1927:

I. The Italian nation is an organic whole, having life, purposes, and means of action superior in power and duration to those of the individuals, single or associated, of which it is composed. It is a moral, political and economic unity, which is realized integrally in the Fascist State.

II. Work in all its forms—intellectual, technical or manual—whether organization or execution—is a social duty. And for this reason only it is regulated by the State. The process of production, from the national point of view, is a single whole; its aims are united and identified with the well-being of the producers and the promotion of national power.

Corporatist doctrine does not aim, of course, to restore the guilds and corporations that flourished in the Middle Ages, but to organize trades and professions in compulsory structures where masters and workers will be permanently linked. Opposed to liberal anarchy, it is also opposed to class war. In the Corporations, conditions of work are supposed to be determined by collective agreements between workers' and employers' representatives which are held to apply to the whole trade, and differences are arbitrated by labor courts within the corporative structure itself. From the economic point of view, Corporatism tends to be restrictive and aims to discipline production. Producers are protected against excessive competition (among other ways, by regulating access to the trade), consumers by price and quality controls. Eventually, Parliament is to be replaced by a Corporative Chamber, representing the coun-

try's economic interests rather than a set of disparate
ideologies and factions. Private property and enterprise
are not directly threatened, but the role of the employer,
of the manager, is envisaged as a social function and he is
held responsible towards the men whom he employs and
towards the community as a whole. As a rule, power will
follow function: if management and ownership are disso-
ciated, the owners who do not actually head an enterprise
may well continue to draw profits but will have less and
less to say about the socially significant part of business
activity—policy and production. Eventually such idle owners are fated to disappear.

"The well-being of producers and the promotion of
national power": social efficiency is the core of the Corporatist doctrine, and this for a good historical reason.
The Corporatist operates in an impoverished and sharply
competitive world in which the margin for error is much
less than it was in the fat 19th century. Now, the wages of
inefficiency may be the death of the nation. In this kind of
world, solidarity appears as the reflection of universal
insecurity, and each nation must learn (or must be taught)
to face the outer world as a tight-knit unit, making the
most of limited resources, achieving the maximum effect
in a restricted space and with restricted means. "There is
a liberty in peacetime which does not exist in war," said
Mussolini in a speech of 1927: "There is a liberty in times
of prosperity which cannot be conceived in a time of
poverty."

In this state of siege, the nation's forces must be mobilized—"polarized," as Manoilescu puts it, "in the service of
a single ideal." And this ideal, to be found in the nation,
is shaped by the directions and the traditions discernible
in the nation's past, which one extrapolates from its history
into the future. Such an ideal cannot be one of individual
freedom, free enterprise, and enlightened self-regard because such concepts are disintegrating and divisive; whereas
the Fascist seeks that which will unify: a group ideal which
will encourage the individual to transcend his private interests and give, abandon, and devote himself to the greater
good of the greater whole. It follows that the national
ideal must be on a grandiose and inspiring scale: imperial,
exciting, theatrical, emotionally satisfying. Without it, no

nation can survive for long: "If a nation has not got [*an ideal*] it must invent it," writes Manoilescu: "For national solidarity becomes a reality to the extent to which the nation serves a common ideal. National idealism thus appears as the first imperative of the 20th century."

Who shall provide the organic integration of national forces, the economic and social organization of the national potential, the invention and assertion of a national ideal? Private individuals are too small for such a task; only the state can do it—a new kind of state, aware of its responsibility as organizer, leader, and inspirer of the nation—a prophet and a pilot all at once. The prototype of this new state that Manoilescu calls *"L'Etat porteur d'ideaux:* the State provider of ideas," is the Fascist state, and on this score the Fascist view is properly Hegelian. "The State," writes a corporatist theorist, "is no longer an instrument for the conservation of individuals and the achievement of their ends; on the contrary, individuals become means, instruments of the life of the State." This view would be forcibly expressed by Mussolini himself before the Fascist Party Congress of 1929: "The individual exists only insofar as he is *in* the State and subordinate to the necessities of the State; the more complex the forms of civilization become, the more freedom of the individual is restricted."

The great difference between the Hegelian and the Fascist states is that the former was really conceived as something divinely willed—a worldly incarnation of a Platonic ideal in process of realization; whereas the latter appears as something of a fraud—the merely pragmatic manipulator of ideas and techniques considered appropriate in certain political circumstances. There is nothing metaphysical, nothing ultimate, about the Fascist state or its ideas. They are intended and, if necessary, invented to work; any pretense that they are more than relative seems to arise from the needs or the excitement of the moment. If a national ideal is lacking, one must be invented. If too many ideals jostle and cause confusion, that one must be selected which best suits the moment. The doctrine is tactical; the tactics are pragmatic and self-consciously so. This explains Mussolini's assertion that Fascism never had a theory or doctrine but invented its philosophy after the fact—after it came to power: the philosophy was not a rationalization, but a systematization, a necessary part of staying in power. An effective political movement needs no ideology because it moves; but an effective state needs one to provide the unifying force and a sense of direction. (*See Reading No. 1C.*)

The Corporatist ideology Mussolini eventually adopted is not necessarily or characteristically Fascist; what is characteristic is Fascism's pragmatic readiness to adopt it because the needs of a given situation at a given moment were felt to require it. In other words, Fascism is *par excellence* pragmatic: its interest is power, its means tend to be violent largely insofar as violence works, its ideas are chiefly negative: the anti-liberalism, anti-individualism and anti-democracy it shares with other and less revolutionary movements, nationalism being the only positive factor.

It was this nationalism that caused the perdition of Fascism—this and Mussolini's belief that struggle toughens and purifies a nation as it does a man. Nothing is less certain than the thought that struggle is always beneficial, an impression Mussolini must have derived partly from Sorel, partly from an indiscriminate combination of Nietzsche and Darwin. But first the vocabulary of Fascism and then its foreign policy sought to act upon this misconception. Italians were called to fight the "battle" of the *lira,* of production, or of wheat: "campaigns" were undertaken to dry marshland or build great stadiums and highways. . . . If this had gone no farther, such pacific warfare would have been well enough, though hard on a poor country none the less. But soon Italian economy would flag no longer under colossal building projects, but under the burden of more murderous campaigns, the series of military enterprises that kept the country at war from 1935 to 1945. Abyssinia (1935-1936), Spain (1936-1939), were the preliminaries of a more devastating conflict which Italy need no more have entered than the first world war, and which Mussolini would end hanging head downward, dead, beside the corpse of his mistress similarly upended, on the Piazzale Loretto in Milan.

The question arises in Mussolini's case as in many others, why he could not leave well alone: why, in a position where friends and foes asked him only to sit tight, he had to intervene and drive his country into ruin. There is no telling the power of vanity and human thoughtlessness. But it would seem that the real cause lay deeper: part of the confusion over the true character of Fascism comes from its advocacy of "order"—a term we generally associate with conservatism or reaction. But Fascist order envisages not the *status quo*—or the *status quo ante*—but a more or less definite order of its own. The Fascist leader, now that God is dead, cannot conceive himself as the elect of God. He believes he is elect, but does not quite know of what—presumably of history and obscure natural forces. The elect of God establishes or guards God's order; the Fascist leader seeks a similar justification—but in the absence of ultimate authority, the order is one that he defines himself, based on a historical interpretation of national destiny.

Thus, nationalism is crucial to the Fascist mind; but, as we have seen, the nationalism of the Fascist is dynamic, his people or his country must sink or swim, struggle ahead unceasingly or fail. The Fascist vehicle is not the tank so much as a bicycle equipped with flails on which one must keep moving so as not to fall. Without precise objectives, the Fascist must move forward all the time; but just because precise objectives are lacking he can never stop, and every goal attained is but a stage on the continuous treadmill of the future he claims to construct, of the national destiny he claims to fulfill. Fascist dynamism comes at the price of this, and therein lies its profound revolutionary nature; but also, it seems, the seeds of its eventual fall.

— 7 —

GERMANY

Revolution, according to Joseph Goebbels (1897-1945), can be defined as "a process which, with its own dynamism

and its own standards, tries to instill into the State the
dynamism and standards which were until then the preserve of the opposition." It would be the purpose of National Socialist revolution to breathe new life into the German state by reaffirming its connection with the people
whose expression it was meant to be, and by establishing
this upon a mixture of concrete measures and of myth
which for some years at least persuaded many Germans
that they were living an extraordinary adventure.

The collapse of the Kaiser's Empire in 1918, the collapse
of the German mark in the early and the middle twenties,
the inflation which destroyed all savings, stocks, and state
bonds, had turned the mass of the German middle class
(so disciplined, so scrupulous, class-conscious, and law
abiding) into economically and socially displaced persons.
The depression which hit Germany as the twenties ended
knocked the last nail into the coffin of a disintegrating order. By 1932, a country of 65 million had 6 million unemployed and 21 million living wholly or in part on
charity or relief. In this swarming mass of unemployed,
the ruined "bourgeois" and "sometime-bourgeoisified proletarians" were united by a common helplessness and
exasperation that drove them into the ranks of the extremist
parties, be they Communists or National Socialists.

Hitler and the Nazis. The latter movement had been
born in postwar Munich, among a crowd of ephemeral
anti-Communist groups, and was named the German Workers' Party. (*See Reading No. 2A.*) In September 1919,
still only half a dozen strong, the German Workers were
joined by the man who made them famous: Adolf Hitler
(1889-1945). As an impoverished youth in the Vienna of
Lueger and Franz-Joseph, Hitler had made up his mind to
rise above a proletariat which he despised for dragging
through the mud "the Nation, the Fatherland, and the
authority of the laws," and to transcend a time "favorable
only to merchants and quill-drivers," where misery co-
existed with the luxury of the business and noble classes,
and with the antideluvian pomp of the Habsburg court.

The way to counter the injustice and decay that young
Hitler saw in Vienna was not the one preached by the
followers of Marx, for Marxism was no better than death,
a "vitriolic" doctrine of selfishness and hatred; and, since

the Austrian Marxists and much of the Austrian press were
said to be led by Jews, the Jewish people seemed to Hitler
the carriers of Marxian decay, a twentieth-century variant
of what he saw as their secularly destructive role. The
feeling that Jews were a foreign body in all societies and
hence destructive would reach in Hitler a pitch of intensity
usually associated with madness: "If the Jew, with his
Marxism, were to win, the earth would become a planet
bare of men as it was millions of years ago." Although the
fierceness of his beliefs disgusted some, it seems to have
had a convincing effect on others, helping to turn his arguments into invocations, the more impressive for being less
coherent and closed to critical examination.

The outbreak of the First World War found Hitler in
Munich where, thanking heaven on his knees for letting
him live in such times, he volunteered for the Bavarian
infantry in which he found the fighting "unforgettable and
sublime." The end of the war found him decorated and
wounded several times. Back in Bavaria, his eloquence, his
violent patriotism, and his fanatical hatred of Marxists,
Jews, and parliamentary institutions won him sympathies
in certain—largely reactionary—political and military
quarters, horrified by the very moderate social-democracy of Weimar.

They would have been more horrified by the agitator
whom they helped to notoriety (for Hitler alone had helped
himself to power); the people that Hitler gathered around
him were far more radical than either the conservative
gentry or the almost equally conservative trade unionists
whom his followers were to displace. To the apocalyptic
promises of Communist revolution, the National Socialists
opposed an apocalypse of their own, capable of galvanizing
the disillusioned and the desperate into an unity for which
they yearned. The faith that held them together was based
on the three ideas of race, folk community, and leadership.

The Leader and the Race. Racial theories are not
peculiar to National Socialism (*see Reading No. 2C*):
partly as a by-product of 19th-century ideas of national
selection, partly under the impact of equally 19th-century
attempts to combine history and sociology in would-be
scientific theories, a great many Germans (including Jew-

ish intellectuals like Walter Rathenau) had come to believe in the existence of "races" with different inherent moral and physical characteristics, and also in the superiority of northern or Aryan peoples. This superiority could only be affirmed and maintained if the characteristics and the purity of the race were not adulterated, as those of Germanic peoples had unfortunately been for a long time by foreign influences and foreign blood. The race had now to be purged of pernicious elements by which it had allowed itself to be infiltrated, and German salvation lay in the recapture (or achievement) of the ideal biological type in which the German race could find fulfillment.

The roots and inspiration for such a revival, a return to the nation's vital sources, could be rediscovered in the secular folk community that blood, soil, and history had created and in the institutions which peculiarly German conditions had forged—religious, social, and economic. The Germans were anarchic and divided because they lived in an artificial society that had lost all sense of community in its institutions and in its laws. A new consciousness of common race, the true democracy of a revived corporative order, would reunite them. But the unifying factor *par excellence* would be the person of the leader, upon whom all aspects of the faith could focus.

The leader does not hold his position because of any particular intellectual or moral superiority, but by a mystic preselection; he is not so much the representative of his people as its medium. Ideally, the leadership principle should be applied at every level in a great cat's cradle of relationships in which each group (families, schools, factories, professions) has its leader, all finding place in a great pyramid of responsibilities and loyalties topped by the national leader. The group cannot be fully united, fully effective, fully *itself*, without the leader who helps it to crystallize, just as he himself is nothing without the group; so the two can only prosper and rise together. The members of the group give up their personal freedom to follow the leader, but gain in effectiveness as a group and in the satisfaction of their will to power, more than they lose as private agents. The relationship is not recorded in a contract, not even reflected in a reasoning process, but similar to the selection of pirate and robber chiefs or that of certain military castes in which a bond of honor and mutual devotion unites the leader to the men he leads.

The notion of race evoked familiar echoes in the minds of the German bourgeoisie; that of the folk community had the attraction of a certain romantic Socialism; the last, that of the leader, fused all this in a group relationship and a hierarchy based on virtues different from those on which position in society heretofore depended. A new, biological democracy (what one of Rathenau's killers called "pleb-iscitary mass-democracy") would take the place of the unreal and ineffective order where no one was really equal because unfair moral, intellectual, or economic differences set them apart. The Nazi Siegfried looked back to the equalitarian elitism of Sparta, to the barracks of the Prus-sian army, to the ideals of a classless society that some French revolutionaries had entertained: in the new order, not property but physical excellence would make for supe-riority; not class but comradeship would provide the basis of the new peer groups; not contract but confidence would create the texture of social and political relationships.

The party creates the conditions in which this Siegfried may be born and thrive; it also manipulates the machinery of the state, which appears in turn as "the secular arm of the German community." The community judges the state by its plebiscites, the state must form its policies to express the profound tendencies, "the general will" of the nation, and the nation is purified, educated, and trained by the party. The party state must intervene in every aspect of public and private life (hence the totalitarian state) because, as Carl Schmitt writes, "any activity is potentially political and thus subject to political decisions" and, furthermore, "it is as a political animal that man can be grasped in his totality and his existential essence."

These were the theories which after 1930 would attract millions of German voters to the Nazi side. As the Nazi regime progressed, the distinction between civil and mili-tary society grew less. The German people were increasingly enlisted in a pan-German crusade not only at the expense of the Jews, but also of other groups or institutions (espe-cially religious) with particularist claims, whose influence might affect the Nazis' monopoly in training the German soul for the fulfillment of its destiny. The opposition that such encroachments met was slight: the soldiers saw in the mobilization of the nation a source of power for themselves, the businessmen a source of profits, the bureaucrats the fulfillment of their dreams of total organization. Gradually, "fundamental laws" created the "unitary, authoritarian, popular" state that Hitler had in mind. The Reichstag, which met seldom and then only to endorse official policy, was completely subordinated to the government, which combined executive and legislative power. The Third Reich, founded on the principle of authority, was ruled by executive decisions and by plebiscites. Between the leader and the nation, said the doctrine, a bond exists: the leader must act to fulfill his duties and account to the people for what he has done; the people must endorse or reject his policies in direct consultations. Meanwhile, the party, depositor of the fundamental principles of National Socialism, present at every level of administrative, professional, and family life, served as a continuous means of contact, applying the directives of the leader, but also keeping him apprised of the popular mood.

Organized Autarky. Forceful but didactic, the Nazi conquest of Germany was relatively gradual; this appears most clearly in their handling of economic problems which affected every aspect of German life. To come to power legally as leader of the most numerous party in the Reichstag (before it became the only one), Hitler combined the destruction of the political structure which he found (dissolution of political parties, taking over of the unions, unification of the federalist Republic by suppression of local sovereignties and establishment of a central national administrative and police structure) with a socio-economic policy more cautious than Nazi theory implied.

The Nazis' economic theorist, Gottfried Feder, had postulated the suppression of interest (and thus of private credit transactions), nationalization of great enterprises, control of smaller ones, state financing of great public works destined to apply the rule that everyone had both the duty and the right to work and a self-sufficient socialist economy, divorced from the influence of private capital—whether German or foreign. The electorate had seemed to like these ideas, but big business naturally did not, nor would German industry have benefited from an approach that favored small and medium enterprises. Such concepts, therefore, were soon abandoned, and Hitler adopted more empirical policies.

The results of the new economic policies, under the able direction of Dr. Schacht and with the power of a forceful and stable state, were impressive: over 6 million unemployed in 1933, were reduced to 4 million in 1934, 2.9 million in 1935, and 300,000 in 1938. National revenue rose from 45 billion marks in 1932 to 61 billion in 1936; national production increased from about 38 billion marks in 1932 to about 75 billion in 1938 (during which time the general production index passed from 52 to 96); the volume of trade rose 25% between 1935 and 1939. Nor did the production of guns unduly hamper the production of butter, whose consumption rose from 483,000 tons in 1932 to 600,000 in 1938 while that of fats, in general, rose correspondingly.

But it is worth remembering that if Feder's ideas were relegated to ideological discussions, over the years the tendency of the empirical measures in whose favor they had been set aside was in his direction. Interest would never be eliminated, nor would the profit motive, but the state which held nearly 70% of the capital of German banks, controlled their activities as it did those of heavy industry by its great holding companies. Import, exchange and price controls allowed the Ministry of National Economy to direct production, distribution, and consumption. Investments would be regulated by the great professional boards that functioned within the complicated structure of the corporate state. Some enterprises were nationalized; other nationalized enterprises were created; no new firms could be set up without special permission. In a short time a great part of the population had been reintegrated into the production circuit, both as producers and consumers, with full employment making a reality of the right to work and voluntary (eventually compulsory) labor for the young making it a duty. In *The Decline of the West*, published in 1917, Oswald Spengler had called on German youth to turn their backs on the effete refinements of decaying civilization and to adopt a peculiarly German morality of effort and of work. No longer the object of haggling or of contracts, a man should treat his work as a joyous, voluntary, community service. Working for the community, that is for themselves, men could accept the necessary disciplines of work as self-imposed and view their labor's product as a common gain. This was very well, if workers could be shown that the product of their labors did in fact benefit them; and Nazis made great efforts to succeed in this. One of the duties of the Labor Front (which incorporated the tasks of the old unions) was to provide satisfactions and rewards for every class of worker (e.g., the well-known and ridiculously inexpensive holidays and cruises of "Strength through Joy"). On the eve of war the Labor Front was spreading its activity into every sphere, from sport and travel to socialized medicine (already existent in Germany) and labor courts. In 1938 alone, factory social services sponsored by the Front as part of its activities employed 26,000 doctors, sent 600,000 children to the countryside, and paid maternity allowances to 150,000 mothers.

A first step towards the autarkic economy which Feder advocated had been taken in 1931, when Germany had established exchange control and removed its currency from free international circulation. Soon after taking power, the National Socialists completed this particular move by abandoning the gold standard and basing the mark's rate on its commercial value in the international market—that is, the demand for marks by people wanting German services and goods. Such a step implied either a favorable trade balance, or a trade policy largely based on barter. Both were tried. In 1933, the figure of imports and exports had fallen respectively from the 1120 and 1124 million marks of 1929 to 350 and 400 million. By 1939, the relevant figures were 456 and 493 million marks. Trade volume had risen 25% since 1935. Exports were exceeding imports, and the situation was healthy enough. In the vital sphere of foodstuffs, although Germany remained dependent on imports for fats, fodders, and colonial products, imports of agricultural produce had fallen from 30% of the total in 1932 to only 17% in 1938, as fallow lands were halved and farmers were given every encouragement to grow more. Meanwhile, important barter agreements had been signed with a number of countries in Eastern Europe and overseas, which furnished essential raw materials. The German economy faced serious problems (arising largely from increased consumption), but its capacity of solving these problems also improved.

It may be that the obsession with self-sufficiency provided an argument for Hitler's policy of conquest, but the argument by itself cannot have been a major one. The needs for self-sufficiency that his policy implied did however lead, especially after the resignation of Dr. Schacht in 1938, to the hardening and progress of state direction as well as regulation of the country's economic life. Henceforth, Article I of the notorious decree of December 1, 1936, would be put into practice: "Any German resident who, consciously or unconsciously, moved by base selfishness or by whatever vile sentiment, contravenes legal rules and causes grave prejudice to German economy, may be condemned to death and his fortune confiscated."

By 1943, the money market as motor of industrial activity had been replaced by the state's planning organizations, the vestiges of capitalism by a planned economy which, unlike in the West, fitted perfectly with National Socialist conceptions, being only the fulfillment of earlier moves. The "German Socialism," soft-pedaled in the middle thirties, was again coming into its own in the form of state capitalism. Political and economic pressures were forcing the Nazis to affirm it at the expense of the business and capital interests they had begun by trying not to offend too much.

Apart from obsessive fanaticism, and from the resentment of middle-class business and professional men against their abler, more successful Jewish competitors, anti-Semitism appeared in the 1930's as an ideal outlet for the anti-capitalist tensions of the mob which the Nazis themselves had done so much to rouse. But once the Jewish minority was eliminated, the essence of that "vagabond and cosmopolitan fortune" which it suited the Nazis to identify with the Jews would be exposed as something else and something more—far more—than Jewish. On the other hand, the Nazi power would feel strong enough to challenge it head on. There seems to be little question that, as happened in Italy, the grip of the dynamic totalitarian state would not have spared the private interests which had helped it secure power.

In the event, the Nazis did not win. But at the very moment of defeat the doctrinaire quality of their beliefs stood out most sharply. Over and over again, the primacy of doctrine over pragmatic logic kept the Germans from using their hard-pressed resources to the full. It was to an important extent principle that kept them from using Russian—especially Ukrainian—hostility against the Communists as they might. It was the same insane principles which used rolling stock the army needed to ship Jews and Gypsies to their slaughter.

The Germans were waging a religious war: they benefited from the fervor this provided; they also paid its price. Nations in our time seem caught in a strange dilemma: without a cause to fight for, they see little reason to fight— even to defend themselves—persuaded that in the end merely material gains hardly outbalance the possibility of death. Only a faith will keep men together in great stress or make them brave great dangers. But for a faith men will do the most savage things: no beastliness is worse than that which great ideals seem to justify in their perpetrators' eyes.

The Germans murdered a people for a dream, a strange dream which fanatical purpose turned to nightmare. And this is the paradox we find in all these movements born in crisis: the crisis calls for action, but also for more than action—it calls for a faith which will make violent and sustained action possible, a faith which will instill the state with the dynamism and standards that we associate more with the opposition, "the party of movement," than with the party in power, which generally guards an established order. But then this faith, in turn, may lead to crimes. And if, as in the case of Hitler, the faith is limitless, both in its undefined aims and in its force, then there need be no end to crimes which are not carried out for a limited purpose so that, once attained, the crimes themselves may cease; but must go on making bloody history forever.

HUNGARY

Patriotic Reactions. The disintegration of the Habsburg monarchy in 1918 left Hungary isolated and beleaguered, retaining less than a third of the territories she had once ruled: of 282,870 square kilometers she kept 91,-174, and of a population of 18 million only 8 million were left. The brief Communist regime of Bela Kun, dislodged by Romanian troops, was succeeded in 1919 by a right-wing reaction, the red terror by a white terror, which settled down by 1920 to the highly conservative rule of aristocratic cabinets headed mostly by great landed magnates. Two attempts of Emperor Charles of Habsburg to seize his crown were repulsed in March and October 1920. Hungary remained a monarchy, but one from which the king continued to be excluded, and where the memories of Saint Stephen's crown were preserved in the person of the regent, a former Austro-Hungarian admiral, Miklos Horthy.

In this rump of an empire, ruled by a former imperial aristocracy, socially displaced persons formed an important group: ex-officers of the Imperial Armies, teachers and administrators who had been employed in large numbers in territories now within Yugoslav, Czech or Romanian borders, refugees from these lands and, in time, students—many of humble origins, turned out by high schools and universities in greater numbers than before the war. All these responded to the Irredentist appeal of a Magyar nationalism exacerbated by defeat. Unrelenting Irredentism—Hungary's claim to the lands she had lost—would be the leading theme of all Hungarian politics after the treaty of St. Germain (1919).

Against this background a number of patriotic societies sprang up, many of them secret. All aimed to reverse the verdict of the war and to restore Hungary's past greatness. The first of these societies and movements was organized in 1918-1919, among the anti-Bolshevik forces who were concentrated in south-eastern Hungary, around the town of Szeged near the Serbian border; their point of view be-

came known as the "Szeged idea"—an idea or, rather, a set
of attitudes, which would be basic to all later nationalist
or Fascist movements that the country would know between the wars. Having lost all they had in revolution or in
flight, most of the representatives of the Szeged idea felt no
particular respect for property and inclined to believe that
the greater part of Hungary's wealth was in the hands of big
landlords and Jews, for whom they bore no sympathy. They
were anti-Semitic because they equated the Jews with exploitation and the money power; and also because many
of the radical intellectuals of the liberal Karolyi government of 1918 and many more of the Commissars of Bela
Kun's red republic of 1919 were alleged to have been Jews.
Above all, they were counter-revolutionary and, naturally,
anti-Bolshevik, wanting to defend Hungary's borders
against the foreigner and protect her internal stability
against the revolution.

The stability which they envisaged, however, was not that
of the old order. In many respects these nationalists of
Szeged could be described as leftists, and they might so
have described themselves if the term had not been smeared
for them by its associations with Socialism, internationalism,
and Jews. Instead, they called themselves "right-wing," or
"right radicals." This, Professor Macartney tells us, was
going to have peculiar consequences: "The ultra-conserva-
tive landed and big business interests were left without an
appropriate label. Hungarians not infrequently called them
'Left' and the English pen, which boggles at following the
example, is left at a loss for an alternative."

Gömbös. The representative leader of these right radicals, whose programs and methods came very close to those
of the radicals of the Left, would be Gyula Gömbös (1886-
1936), born in a Swabian district, the son of a schoolteacher who may well have been of German stock and of
a local farmer's daughter who did not speak Hungarian at
all. Like many people of doubtful descent (Degrelle's
father's family came from the region of Maubeuge in
France, his mother's family from German Moselle; Codreanu's father, named Zelinsky, was Polish or Ruthenian;
Hitler, of course, was an Austrian) Gömbös early became
a truculent Hungarian nationalist. A captain in the war, at
Szeged he had been appointed Minister of Defense and,

after Horthy's regime had been securely established, he resigned from the army to become a politician, the chief spokesman of the Szeged idea and, for the last four years of his life, prime minister of his country.

Gömbös spoke of himself as a Hungarian National Socialist as early as 1919, and he took his National Socialism very seriously, although it meant in part war against the false Socialism of Marxism: "a destructive heresy foisted on simple workers by self-seeking international Jews." Opposed to corrupting Marxism, he was however just as opposed to landlords and to financiers, attacking inherited privileges and the caste system, favoring radical land reform, and declaring that he recognized no difference between classes. He once shocked Parliament by affirming that his generation had no use for counts unless they worked, "when they would be treated like everybody else," and he carried these principles into practice in 1932 by forming the first Hungarian cabinet which did not include a single count.

As early as 1921, his anti-Semitism and his Irredentist conspiracies brought Gömbös into contact with like-minded groups in Munich (where Hitler was then busy as an obscure hanger-on), including the original National Socialist Workers' Party, White Russians, Ukrainians, and German and Bavarian nationalists. But Gömbös did not like the Germans, and his vaguely social-patriotic ideas developed into a doctrine only in the late twenties under the impact of Mussolini, from whom (despite the Fascists' regrettable lack of anti-Semitism) he seems to have borrowed the idea of leadership in an integrated corporative state.

As Gömbös rose to power in the early thirties, his policies—in which even the anti-Semitism had been toned down by the necessities of government—became too moderate for a new generation whose Socialism and Nationalism were more uncompromising. The high school and university graduates of the postwar years cared nothing for the social system which their parents and their conservative rulers still accepted. "Some of the most penetrating and also the most radical works on Hungarian social conditions," writes Macartney, "came from men who were afterwards penalised as war criminals and their works burned as Fascist." Yet such men could not gravitate to-

wards the classic Left. For one thing, the position was still
identified with the antinational revolution of 1918-1919.
For another thing, it was uncomfortable: the Communist
party had been outlawed and the Social-Democrats were
far too liberal and internationalistic for the young men's
taste. Also, the Left was not anti-Semitic, whereas the
middle classes were profoundly so, both by prejudice and
by economic considerations, the Jews seeming to bar their
way in many businesses and liberal professions.

Although anti-Semitism kept many radicals from going
Left, it also kept them from the conservative Government
Party, whose economic ties with Jews were too close and
whose prejudices were too weak for it to countenance any
serious anti-Semitic action. Their sympathies would go to
the Nationalist Socialist parties of the thirties. The latter,
however, drew much of their rank and file support from
the urban and rural proletariat—a class to whom anti-
Semitic appeals meant little, but radical reform meant a
good deal. Thus Hungarian National Socialist appealed to
the middle classes by their anti-Semitism and to the workers by their radicalism. And a great many radicals of the
Right, who wanted to change the whole political and social
structure of the nation, would find in Nazism as they saw
it across the German border—and quite apart from its
anti-Semitism—the hope for drastic remedies which middle-
class reformers had promised but failed to carry out.

The political parties that sprang up in the thirties are
easily confused because they bore similar labels, were often
amalgamated only to split again, or disappeared to revive
under another name: Scythe Cross or National Socialist
Party of Labor, which simply took over the Nazi program
(1931); the Hungarian National Socialist Agricultural
Laborers' and Workers' Party, with its brown shirts and its
green swastika on a brown field (1932); the Hungarian
National Socialist People's Party (1933), and the Hitlerite
National Socialist Party which imitated the whole Nazi
pattern from swastika to jackboots (1933), and then some
more. By 1934, the chief formations had adopted the distinctive marks of Hungarian National Socialism: the green
shirt and the Arrow Cross badge. Soon they would crystallize around the person of one man: Ferencz Szalasi (1897-
1944).

Szalasi. Szalasi's ancestors came of Armenian stock,
for many Armenians had immigrated into Transylvania in
the 18th century. But his grandfather, who moved to
Vienna, found a small job on the railways, and chose an
Austrian wife, had changed his name from Salosjan or
Salojian to a more Hungarian consonance. Ferencz's father
had been a noncommissioned officer in the imperial army;
his mother was of mixed Hungarian and Slovak origin.
Ferencz, after serving in the war, entered the Hungarian
army and was appointed to the General Staff in 1925 where
he soon gained the reputation of being a "military revolutionary." He studied politics and sociology and read Marx,
Bebel, Kropotkin, Lenin, and Trotsky so thoroughly that
he was always able to quote passages from their works. He
investigated the possibilities for action of the opposition
parties (including the Social-Democrats) and resigned from
the army in 1934 to devote himself to political activity.

Szalasi's great idea was "Hungarism," the dream of uniting the peoples of the "Great Carpathian-Danubian Fatherland" with the peoples from Ruthenia to the Adriatic, a
kingdom where the Magyars would be dominant (as the
chosen people) but not exclusive. The first instrument for
the realization of this ideal would be the Party of the National Will, which he founded in 1935, dedicating it to
"the Trinity of Soil, Blood and Work," and then the Arrow
Cross Party, which he set up to succeed it. (*See Reading
No. 3A.*)

Szalasi's dream of the triumph of Hungarism took precedence over whatever means he could find to fulfill it. The
Party's purpose was to carry him—the leader—to power;
but this power was to be achieved (and Szalasi insisted on
this and remained true to it) "by the common will of the
nation and of the Head of the State." For Szalasi wanted
to take power by constitutional means—against the existing
parliamentary parties, certainly, which did not derive their
power from the freely expressed will of a people who had
never seen free elections, let alone a secret ballot; but not
against the people themselves, nor against their constitutional head, the regent, Horthy.

"The people" were crucially important not only as the
many-headed symbol of national reality, but also because
Szalasi realized that their support was crucial in the event
of war. At such times everything had to go with perfect

smoothness and national resources had to be exploited to
their utmost; one could not risk the chaos of even a 24-hour
strike. Essential to national security as to the national welfare, the workers must not be allowed to "be led astray, on
account of material or ideological questions, into paths dangerous and fatal to the State." Social justice was important,
but social integration was more important still. Workers
had to be taught that they were one with the state, their
state, "so that when the hour came they would identify
themselves with it and work to realize its objectives as their
own."

Marxism was powerful and impressive, but it overlooked
national interests for class interests, and it took its orders
from Moscow. The barren materialism of Marxism could
bring Hungary nothing; the equally materialistic slogans of
a weak liberalism which the people knew largely as the
harbinger of injustice provided no satisfactory rejoinder.
The only match for Marxism lay in National Socialism,
with which Szalasi appealed to the workers with some effect.
In the election of May 1939, the first to be conducted
with a secret ballot, various National Socialist groups won
48 out of 259 parliamentary seats. Thirty-one of these seats
went to Szalasi's Arrow Cross. Though holding less than
a fifth of the seats, the National Socialists had received
750,000 of the two million votes cast, and in Budapest their
72,383 votes compared favorably with the Government
Party's 95,468. Just outside the capital, Czepel, which
was also known as Red Czepel because it boasted the
greatest industrial concentration in the country, elected two
National Socialists.

Mistrusted by the Hungarian conservatives because of his
ambitions and his revolutionary program, unable to come
to an understanding with the Nazis because of his uncompromising Hungarist principles, Szalasi could not secure
either the support of the moderate regent or that popular
endorsement without war for which he hoped. Hungary's
alliance with Fascist Italy in 1927 had been signed by
conservatives; it was conservatives who negotiated with
Hitler in 1938, 1940, and thereafter; and conservatives
again who, in the early months of 1944, delivered to the
Germans the greater part of Hungary's Jews.

The Arrow Cross, however, made its influence indirectly
felt: largely under its pressure, conservative governments

reluctantly started distributing land to the peasants. More significantly, in trying to counteract the party's vigorous activity—which, according to a French observer, was winning sympathies "not only in the country proletariat, but among students, poor intellectuals and officers"—Gömbös's successors adopted many of its essential points and methods. Thus, even though the Arrow Cross remained out of power, its ideas left their mark on the Hungarian political and intellectual scene.

Even Szalasi's imprisonment, in the late thirties, for anticonstitutional activities, did not prevent the Arrow Cross's parliamentary representation increasing, and its ideas shifting the center of gravity of the conservative government coalition well towards the Right. Meanwhile, left to his lieutenants, the party had begun to flourish on German money and, while the Arrow Cross became known as a "German" party, it also welcomed Communist supporters. (In the elections of 1940, the Communist Party was to tell its followers to vote for it.) Soon the Arrow Cross was riven between opportunistic pro-Nazis who blamed Szalasi for tolerating Communists and, even more, for refusing all concessions to the Germans and, on the other side, radical members who accused him of forgetting the party's old social program.

What everyone had forgotten was that social program or political maneuvers had been for Szalasi merely aspects of a much wider dream. In its pursuit, and after being freed from prison, the leader purged his party as well as he could, of both the opportunists and Communists even though this meant losing a great deal of strength in parliament and in the country. However, Szalasi, unmoved by such mundane considerations, was busy working out plans for the eventual organization of his Hungarist Corporatist State—including such refinements, Macartney tells us, as a compulsory anthropological examination for all officials. By the end of 1943, when membership had sunk below 100,000 and the party's spirits were very low, Szalasi worked out plans for an Institute of Racial Biology. The following summer he sent Hitler elaborate plans for a tribal reorganization of Europe. Momentary difficulties did not worry him; he felt certain that his time would come, and it soon did.

Hungary had been dragged into war much against her

will, by German pressure and by her military leaders' ambitions. At the beginning of 1944, unsuccessful efforts to get the country out of the conflict led to the German occupation of the country, the suppression of all but right-wing parties, and an influx of new members into the Arrow Cross. And, while the middle classes and the army contributed their share, workers were not the least numerous among those who joined it. Szalasi's had been the only right-wing movement seriously to bother with (and about) the workers: although many, of course, clung to Socialism or entered the Communist underground, a goodly number joined the Arrow Cross.

Szalasi's own reaction to the new circumstances was characteristic: his was the only party to demonstrate and scatter leaflets against the German occupation and against the collaborating Sztojay government which obeyed them. Szalasi himself was willing to take power, "by will of the people," and to lead the nation against Bolshevism, but on condition that the Germans integrally accept his Hungarist ideas and give his policy full rein. The Germans, like most Hungarian politicians, thought he was crazy: they preferred to deal with other National Socialist groups whose policy consisted largely of anti-Semitism and collaboration. But, while rejecting cooperation with other factions of this subservient Right, vigorous Arrow Cross propaganda was making converts among the working classes; and the prophet's hour came at last when, in October 1944, Horthy, negotiating for an armistice, was forced to abdicate and interned by Germans, and Szalasi was in power.

While waiting for this moment, the leader had prepared a complex plan to organize the nation into corporations, nationalize mines and power stations, place industry and trade under state control, mechanize agriculture and break the money power's hold upon it, employ the Jews on public works, and then settle them elsewhere after the war. "The Corporatist Order of the Working Nation" kept the new head of state and his ministers busy; but little could be done to implement it, for Hungary had been overrun by Russian armies and Budapest was soon encircled in a siege that was to last until the end of winter.

While the troops fought and the city starved, while bands of hooligans and Arrow Cross militia tortured and mas-

sacred Jews and political opponents, Szalasi himself "retired completely into the clouds," dictating his memoirs,
commandeering newspaper presses to print Arrow Cross
theoretical works, attending seances where optimistic spirits
predicted the downfall of the Western powers. His mind, almost unhinged, dwelt in spheres of high policy and con-
stitution-making far removed from the desperate situation
of that bloody winter. Before long he would be tried and
executed by the victors for the acts of treason and terror
committed in his name. The man, however, was neither
brute nor traitor but, as Macartney puts it, a person "of the
most unyielding principles, on which he insisted with a
maddening monotony and a rigidity which rejected the
slightest compromise." Even with reality: the man was mad.

— 9 —

ROMANIA

Codreanu. The doctrines of Corneliu Zelea Codreanu
and his Nationalism were of a completely different essence
than that which we discover in other social movements of
our time. While sharing the main traits which we have
found elsewhere, Codreanu's dream drew its inspiration
from an older, Christian tradition and spoke in chiliastic
accents the West had known in the 14th or 16th century but forgotten since. (*See Reading No. 4A.*) Simpler
than the ideologies developed in the West, the ideologies of
Codreanu's Legionaries were also more thoughtful and
in some ways more subtle, because they considered moral
problems that others had ignored. And this was only proper
for a movement which grew up in forests, in monasteries,
and in prisons themselves set up in disaffected cloisters,
among the sons of peasants and of priests, its chief emblem
provided by an icon.

Codreanu's father's name had been Zelinski; his mother came of Protestant German stock. Codreanu was baptized in the Orthodox Church (which is the national church of Romania) at the same time as his parents. While his father taught in a provincial high school, the boy grew up in a military academy in the Moldavian forests. He graduated just as the First World War came to an end—a war which had been hard for Romania, but from which she emerged twice as large as she had been upon her entry. The elation of the postwar years was mitigated by the presence of vindictive neighbors who claimed the territories that had just been annexed: Bulgarians in the south, Hungarians in the west, and above all Russians in the east across the Dniester. Communist propaganda feeding on antiquated conditions in industry and on the land caused disturbances throughout the country.

To young Romanian nationalists, most of whom were poor students or intellectuals, often just up from the land, the economic claims of peasants and of workers were just; they were however confused with Communism which, to the Romanian, seemed one with a Russian imperialism by which the country had long been threatened. And it appeared that a majority of Communist leaders were Jews, a national group which in Eastern Europe far more than in the West appeared as a separate community, set apart by custom, by language and, frequently, by dress. The equation between Jews and Communism, Communism and Russian conquest, hence Jews and the foreign threat, suggested itself at once to the adolescents whom Codreanu gathered around him at the University of Iasi.

The core of historical Romania lies in two provinces: Wallachia in the south, between the Carpathians and Danube, Moldavia in the north, between Transylvania and Bessarabia—both highways for conquerors, traders, and invaders on their way from the Balkans to the Baltic, or from the Russian plains towards the warmer southwest. Bucharest, the country's capital, lies in Wallachia, to the south; Iasi was the chief city of Moldavia and was an old, established cultural center where German, French, and Russian influences met in a widely read bourgeois and student world. Iasi had also been, over the past 50 years, a favorite immigration center for many Russian and Polish

Jews fleeing first tsarist and then bolshevik persecution; local trade, small businesses, and much also of legal and medical practice, seem to have been in Jewish hands.

The dominant figure at the University of Iasi was Professor A. C. Cuza, whose political doctrine resumed itself in violent anti-Semitism. Strongly influenced by the writings of Edouard Drumont, Cuza had been one of a group of young Romanian Socialists who, in 1883, had launched from Brussels the first Romanian Socialist periodical— *Dacia*—which reflected both nationalist and Socialist preoccupations. Cuza's anti-Semitism was not based on the religious prejudices common in Eastern Europe, but on economic considerations. The youthful Socialist became a radical conservative and was inspired more by Maurras's distrust of liberalism and the liberal state than by his earlier Marxian inclinations. By the time Codreanu heard him lecture in the Faculty of Law, the old man was the country's leading anti-Semite, but little else. Nationalism as such scarcely sets a man apart in Romania, where all politicians had made their way largely by nationalist agitation—often in provinces under foreign domination. But in 1923 the country was torn by the government's decision (as bound by the peace treaties from which it had done so well) to grant Romanian citizenship to all resident Jews—a move particularly resented by Moldavians; it was Cuza whom Codreanu and his friends asked to preside over the National Christian Anti-Semitic League (LANC) which they set up.

Murder as Method. The riots fomented by the LANC forced the government to close the universities, and this in turn led to other riots. Eventually, Codreanu and his followers were arrested for planning a murder campaign by which to clear the country, less of the Jews than of their corrupt protectors. Denounced, they would be imprisoned for five months. After a sympathetic trial all were released but one, Ion Moța, who had managed to shoot their denouncer on the very day of the trial and had to await another acquittal at a later date.

Codreanu and his companions then returned to Iasi and apparently gave up any further thought of murders. Inspired by *Narodnik* and Tolstoian ideas then current in Romanian intellectual circles and believing manual labor essential to a balanced mind, they set out to build their own student center with bricks they made themselves and money raised by working in a market garden. But the authorities suspected that their intentions were less pacific than they seemed, and the prefect himself led the gendarmes to break them up with great (and unnecessary) brutality. Arrested without apparent reason at their work, they were dragged through the streets tied up with ropes, spat on, beaten, humiliated, and only released on Cuza's intervention and that of certain leading citizens. Shortly thereafter, Codreanu, who had been denied any hearing for his griefs, let alone any sanctions against the prefect, took the law into his own hands by shooting the official down. Aware that public opinion was on Codreanu's side, the authorities decided to hold his trial away from Iasi: first in another Moldavian town, then at the other end of the country, at Turnu Severin, where Trajan had thrown his bridge across the Danube. But even there the trial turned into a triumph, with trainloads of sympathizers pouring into town, even forcing the tribunal to abandon its courtroom for the local theater, itself hardly sufficient to hold the public. "All we have done, we have done for our country and our faith," declared the accused: "We swear to fight to the end." The jury stayed out exactly five minutes and returned sporting on their lapels the LANC emblem—the national colors with a swastika on top. Codreanu was acquitted and, when he returned to Iasi, the peasants gathered at the wayside to cheer him, while in the cities great crowds filled the railroad stations with flowers and songs.

But the LANC was not going well. Cuza was running the League as if it were a political party. Codreanu had wanted it to be a movement of moral restoration, more like a military order, where what really counted would be spiritual values and readiness to sacrifice self for the cause. In June 1927, with a dozen friends, he left the League and founded the Legion of the Archangel Michael, placed under the patronage of the warrior saint whose icon had caught Codreanu's attention in a prison chapel, and whose image would henceforth preside over his life and that of the movements which he led.

With the help of Mota's father, a priest, the little band put out a magazine, *Land of Our Forefathers,* whose title page carried two quotations. Under the figure of St.

Michael, the first one read: "Ruthlessly I raise my sword against the impure ones who seek to enter the house of God." The other, from a Romanian poet, said: "We are in the hands of God. One only dies once. Be it in the flower of youth, be it very old, death is exactly the same. But it is not the same whether one dies like a lion or like a mad dog."

Within a few days, *Land of Our Forefathers* had 3000 subscribers, and the subscribers of today would be the partisans of tomorrow. The Legion was organized in "Nests" of 13 or less, in which every member had to take an oath: "We bind ourselves before God and men to remain closely united around our leaders, to obey and carry out orders received, to work for the ever deeper popular penetration of the new spirit of Work, Honesty, Sacrifice and Justice, in a world where we want to convert all with whom we come in contact into Legionaries, that is sharers in these beliefs. We believe in God and in the Legion's victory. We believe in a new Romania which we shall conquer through Jesus Christ and through integral nationalism, acting through the country's Legions."

A Puritan Host. The rules for members were laid down in a *Nest Leader's Manual* which Codreanu himself prepared, and which in its thoroughness has been compared to Loyola's *Institutes*. Its dispositions were at any rate appropriate to a talkative, lazy, undisciplined, unreliable, and most unpunctual people:

1. Rule of discipline: be disciplined, for only thus will you win through. Follow your leader through good and evil.

2. Rule of labor: work. Work every day. Put your heart in your work. Let the reward of your work be not gain but the satisfaction that you have done your share to advance the Legion and improve Romania.

3. Rule of silence: speak little. Say what has to be said. Speak when you need. Your oratory is the oratory of the deed. You act; let others talk.

4. Rule of education: you must become *another*. A hero. Let the nest provide all your education. Know the Legion well.

5. Rule of mutual help: help your brother fallen on evil days. Do not abandon him.

6. Rule of honor: follow only the ways that honor suggests. Fight and never be a coward. Leave the ways of infamy to others. It is better to fall fighting with honor than to win through an infamy.

To insist on work, on discipline, and on scrupulous honesty was very important in a society where manual labor was held in low esteem and work of any order best avoided, where truth was at a premium and anarchic corruption was the rule. The Legion set up work camps wherever it could and filled them with volunteers who sometimes crossed a province on foot to get there. It built for itself and for the villages near which it worked; it raised money by marketing produce that it grew; it trained its members in a hard school. The *Manual* also prescribed marches on Sundays and holidays so that members should learn to know their country, the countryside, and the neighboring villages. Marching, said the *Manual,* is healthy and good for the spirit. "But, above all, the march is the symbol of action, of legionary exploration, of the Legion's victory."

It was also a means of bringing the gospel to the peasants, who soon got used to Legion meetings in the churchyard, in which a greenshirted speaker announced that the day of resurrection was at hand, new times were coming, a world without faith was about to disappear and be replaced by another in which everyone would have his place, not according to learning, diplomas, or birth, but to the strength of his faith and the quality of his soul.

In June 1931, the Iron Guard—as Codreanu at first named the movement—won 34,000 votes in national elections: not enough to elect a deputy. Within a few months, however, both Codreanu and his father had been elected to Parliament in Moldavian by-elections and, after the new elections of 1932, four Legionary deputies were seated in Parliament, pledged to turn their representatives' salaries over to the Legion which then allowed them "a minimal sum sufficient to lead a modest life." Meanwhile, the Legion pressed forward in the countryside, building its way into the heart of peasantry and youth, constructing dykes, repairing bridges, churches, schools, and roads. In July 1933, Codreanu told his Legionaries: "The time has come to get to work. Enough of politics, enough of talk. We want to build, from the smallest to the greatest . . . even villages, even cities, even a new Romanian State. The vocation of our generation is to build a new country on the ruins of today." Five months later, a new (Liberal) prime minister, Ion Duca, ordered the Legion dissolved, its centers closed, and its members arrested all over the country. Three weeks later Duca was shot down on a railroad platform. His murderers were sentenced to hard labor, but Codreanu, who had been tried with them, was released to continue his subversion by work. A Legion Labor Corps was at once set up and the dissolved Iron Guard was reformed under a new name: "All for the Fatherland." In the next elections, the party would win 15.58% of the votes and rank as the third largest political formation in the country, but, actually, by far the most popular and the most dynamic.

It would not enjoy this success long. Within two months King Carol II had dismissed his new prime minister, who had been chosen from Cuza's National-Christian Party, and had replaced him with a palace government headed by the Patriarch but actually run by a ruthless but able Minister of the Interior, Călinescu, who proclaimed a new constitution that confirmed Carol's personal dictatorship. His party once more dissolved, Codreanu was arrested together with his chief aides and murdered on government orders while serving a sentence for "treason." Within ten months Călinescu too had been killed, his death to be avenged in turn by the killing, upon Carol's orders, of several hundred imprisoned Legionaries, whose corpses were publicly exhibited *pour encourager les autres*.

The Wages of Violence. Blood had fed on blood, murder had bred more murder, until a movement that had affirmed its legalism and spirituality foundered in a tragic blood bath. Never, Codreanu had written, in a private circular, never would the Legion have recourse to conspiracy or to a *coup d'état*. "The very essence of our thinking is against such methods which we consider far too precipitate and too external; we expect our victory to come from the fulfilment in the nation's soul of a process of human perfectionment." But while the Legionaries tried to employ legal, constitutional means, the government had used its power to break the law it was supposed to represent. This, declared a later *Circular*, had changed the relationship between the Legion and the country's rulers

from one of *right* to one of *force:* "This we do not accept.
We were acting within the law, expressing our beliefs. . . .
If this is forbidden, our party's reason for existence ends.
We want to use force. We want to use violence."

True, violence had marked the Legion's activities from
the very beginning, but violence in a violent country where
the law worked for the party in power and where political
banditry is historically connected with memories of patriot
haiduci that held the foreign occupants to ransom. Legionary murders had been committed to answer offenses
from quarters whose crimes would never come to court.
"The Christian," Professor Nae Ionescu wrote, "must for-
give offenses against himself, but not against God and
against God's law." Further, he must discriminate between
sins of commission and sins of omission, the latter sometimes more serious: for instance, permitting a rogue to
kill an innocent person for fear of intervening. "When,"
quoth the *Manual,* "I have to choose between the death of
my country and that of a thug, I prefer the thug to die and
am a better Christian if I do not let him hurt my country and lead it to perdition."

Such violence, however, must be compensated—expur-
gated—by sacrifice: and here Codreanu's originality appears. Expiation is necessary to re-establish the balance
which violence has broken. Legionary doctrine rejected
what one of them described as the police-style spirit of
darkness in underhand or violent activity. It recognized
that ends could be soiled by means. "Even if he should win,
he will remain defeated because he has used devilish
weapons. His breast must be of iron, but lily-white his
soul," Codreanu would insist: "Any conception that
changes or endangers this aim must be denounced as tending to pervert the Legionary spirit and to render impossible the appearance of the *new man* and the *new world*
the Movement wants to bring about."

The argument with which such a dilemma was resolved
ran in a curious way, and may be found in works of
exegesis published since the war. Since the enemy uses all
the arms of darkness, the Legion as a *political* movement
cannot insist on the absolute purity which it stresses in its
indoctrination. It has to maintain the moral essence of its
values; but it also has to fight. The only way to do this

without giving way to general moral corruption, is for those who are fighting with the enemy's own arms never to forget their sin and to suffer for it always in the privacy of their hearts. "This expiation by suffering constitutes the sacrifice which can re-establish the balance of absolute Legionary purity," explains a Legion theorist. He compares this with the sacrifice of several companies of Legionaries which, while the main body of their movement crosses a narrow pass, detach themselves to engage the enemy ensconced in caves and caverns along the way, where they must fight with weapons suited to such dark recesses. "But their weapons are not the weapons of light. They have lost their candor and their purity. They have had to fight with the arms of darkness. Thanks to them, the mass of Legionaries have crossed the pass unharmed. They have not known the struggle in the gloom. . . . The others [*who have known it*] will have to expiate. . . . Their suffering will uplift both them and the Movement."

Thus, for his followers, the death of Codreanu—the Captain, as they called him—and that of his friends (in November 1938), appeared as a martyrdom which, transcending the forces of evil, had marked the movement with the invincibility of an essential Christianity, "for the true and eternal victory is the victory born of martyrdom."

Unfortunately, Codreanu's martyrdom would not end that of his country or of his followers, and many of the latter would not evince dislike for the realm of darkness. In September 1940, after a brief legionary uprising supported by the army, King Carol abdicated and left Romania. The government was taken over by a coalition of the army, represented by the Premier, General Antonescu, and the Legion, whose "Commander" (and Codreanu's heir), Horia Sima, was vice-premier. But an alliance between the conservative nationalists of the army and the revolutionary nationalists of the Legion could not last. The Legion had hoped for the support of the occupying German "allies," but the Germans were more interested in efficient government than in fellow-National Socialists whose Nationalism (as in Hungary) too often clashed with their own. For several months the two sections of the government waged an underhanded civil war, rival police and gendarmerie arrested opponents or protected their friends, while exasperated legionaries paid off old debts and slaked old spites with guns and knives and axes.

Finally, in January 1941, with the connivance of the Germans, Antonescu proceeded to rid himself of his legionary ministers and prefects. The Legion replied with a bloody insurrection that kept Bucharest in terror for four days, while the occupied radio station dinned out the somber slogan, "Long live Death!" Before the army had crushed the Legion, several thousand of their enemies and of Bucharest's Jewish population had been massacred in their homes, in the streets, and in the city's slaughterhouses, where human victims replaced animal carcasses on the butcher's hooks. By the end of the month the Legion had been broken, its leaders killed, arrested, or in flight. Those of its members who had survived sat out the war in German confinement (held by the Nazis as a service to Antonescu and, perhaps, also as a threat over his head), or else joined to fight in Russia, where they died in droves. Their epitaph had been written by Codreanu: "We do not care whether we shall win, whether we shall be broken, whether we shall die. Our aim is another: to go forward, united, together." But unity is not enough. The question always arises: unity for what? And there the answer always remained purposely vague: "Anybody can draw up a program overnight," said the *Manual.* "That is not what the country needs. Better look for men. Legionaries are the men of a faith—of a great spiritual school—and one can trust them better than men held together by a mere program. For the moment, the Legion's program can be resumed in three points: 1. create force; 2. use this force so as to defeat all opposing forces; 3. then apply the program properly so-called."

But, with the leader dead, the program became difficult to formulate, and the savage forces that the Legion had exalted became harder to hold back. From a means of expiation, death became an end and, transcendence replaced by *Götterdämmerung,* turned high ideals into a sordid doom.

GREAT BRITAIN

From Socialism to Fascism. A Fascist movement in Great Britain seems almost a contradiction because Great Britain—and especially England—is known as a law-abiding and constitution-minded country, where violence is out of place, existing institutions are respected, and gradual reform is the rule. If a Fascism of sorts developed under such circumstances, it was, indeed, because reform seemed much too gradual, too slow to cope with pressing problems the country had to face, too indecisive to save its industrial life from struggle and disastrous collapse.

Like France, Great Britain came out of the war victorious but diminished. Her foreign holdings had been sold to pay for the war, domestic capital had been immobilized in war loans, industrial equipment that had become worn over the years had not been replaced, and postwar United States credits had gone to German firms where interest rates were higher (though payments shortly ceased). After a century or more of economic primacy, the country found it hard to acknowledge its straitened circumstances. As soon as possible, Conservative governments returned to the gold standard which, while strengthening the Pound Sterling, also made it more vulnerable and helped to make British products more expensive, hence less competitive and hard to sell abroad. Yet Great Britain could no longer pay for imports from the revenue of her capital investments abroad, which were now largely liquidated. It had to export to live, and this was difficult on markets, most of which were protected by tariffs designed to foster developing national industries.

To resolve their economic difficulties, the governments could only answer with economies, both in national spending and in industry—which meant salary cuts throughout the public and the private sector, further restriction of investment, and delay in modernizing the industrial plant. These policies created dissatisfaction, which gave rise to grave industrial unrest and strikes in the mid-twenties. The elections of 1929 brought a Labor Government to power under the premiership of a veteran pacifist Socialist, Ramsay MacDonald.

The youngest minister of cabinet rank in the first Labor Government of England was Oswald Mosley (1896-   ), the son of a Lancashire Baronet and landowner. As Chancellor of the Duchy of Lancaster, Mosley was particularly charged with preparing a plan to deal with industrial doldrums and rising unemployment. The question was important; the crash of the New York stock market had followed MacDonald's taking office by only a few months, and unemployment in England was already putting the population of whole towns and villages on relief.

Mosley soon set to work. But Labor politicians were no more radical than their Conservative opponents, and just as reluctant to rock the boat. All suggestions for moves that went against accepted institutions, free trade, free enterprise, a minimum of government interference, were treated with suspicion. We must remember that in Britain, as in other European countries, the carnage of the war had wiped out almost an entire generation. Furthermore, since the country had no compulsory military service for some years, the hecatombs of the first two years had operated selectively against the social and intellectual upper classes, whose young had hastened to volunteer and had been mown down in droves in the great butcheries of the Western front. The Chapels of Oxford and Cambridge colleges bear eloquent witness to the numbers of those who died then, removing most of the elite that in the normal course of events would have replaced or challenged their elders. Thus, with the fathers dead and their sons too young to come into their own until the thirties (a time which saw the rise of a notable group of rebels), the years between the two wars —especially the twenties and the early thirties—were dominated by old men and by mediocrities.

Like families, like businesses, like the literary and artistic world, political parties were led by men of the 19th century, whose age made them timid and reluctant to change. Reform meant adventure; radical reform meant dangerous risks. Within the Labor Party, men who had become accustomed to the oft-repeated formulas of democratic Socialism could not envisage their implications without qualms, and preferred to shelter behind claims of principial purity (all or nothing), which meant doing nothing in practice.

Yet, in a world where tariff walls were closing border after border, a policy of free trade and a convertible Pound Sterling tied to an arbitrary gold standard rather than to a more realistic index of exchange and costs, could only worsen Britain's economic situation. In May 1930, unable to persuade his colleagues to act on his proposals, Mosley resigned from the cabinet; in October, he argued his case before the annual Labor Party Conference, and was only narrowly defeated by the ever-conservative votes of the great Trade Unions (which Henri de Man also found hard to budge at a later date). Two months later he addressed himself to the country in a Manifesto for which he had secured the support of 15 other Labor M.P.'s (Members of Parliament)—among them Aneurin Bevan, John Strachey, J. F. Horrabin—one Independent, and the General Secretary of the British Miners' Federation, A. J. Cook.

Although it expressed the views of the most go-ahead Socialists, this document (published in *The Times* of December 8, 1930) now appears not only remarkably moderate, but also prophetic. It called for an immediate plan to meet the emergency situation, more drastic and determined than anything the government had formulated. It advocated a small emergency cabinet with the power to put through policy unhampered by Parliament, and a national economic planning organization to rationalize the country's sagging industrial structure and adjust the balance of British production. In proposals familiar to readers of Keynes or students of the New Deal, the former not yet widely known, the latter yet to come, it argued that "the resources of the State should be mobilized to assist in the development of new industries, and to secure the modernization and re-equipment of industry, especially in the sphere of electricity and transport." But subvention also meant control: "the rationalization of separate industries must have its complement in the coordination, the balance, and the guidance which only a national planning organization can give."

First among European Socialists, Mosley (and at the

time Bevan and Strachey, too) drew the conclusions which
the economic crisis forced upon internationalist doctrine:

> Before we can plan we must control and regulate the factors
> which prevent the wise direction of our production. The
> home market must be the future basis of British trade, and
> that home market depends on the high purchasing power of
> the people, which in turn depends upon high wages. Purchas-
> ing power can only be maintained and increased if the wages
> and conditions of the workers are sheltered from present
> crisis in the world conditions, such as price fluctuations, or-
> ganized dumping, and the competition of sweated labor.
> Neither the protection nor the free trade of the last century
> is effective for this purpose—a modern machine must be
> created to meet the new situation.

So, imports would be controlled and cheapened by the bulk
purchases of an Import and Price Control Board, production and capital investment would be encouraged by dis-
criminatory taxation, agriculture would be protected against
price fluctuations, housing and social services would be
developed, and public works would be initiated, thus serving society and at the same time putting money into circulation, an autarkic economic structure would be created
and strengthened by the integration and organization of the
Commonwealth's productive possibilities.

"In the advancement of this immediate policy," the
Manifesto's signatories declared, "we surrender nothing of
our Socialist faith. The immediate question is not a question of the ownership but of the survival of British industry.
Let us put through an emergency program to meet the
national danger; afterwards political debate on fundamental
principle can be resumed."

Mosley's Manifesto, Beatrice Webb noted in her diary,
was "an able document . . . and there is much reason for
it." Her husband, Sydney Webb—then Lord Passfield and
a minister in the cabinet which Mosley had left—evidently
did not agree, and neither did the Labor Party from which
Mosley soon resigned to start a New Party of his own,
arguing that one "could not go on shouting the meaningless slogans [*of a 19th-century Socialism*] which has no
more in common with the modern age than crinolines and
whiskers."

That summer, Mosley and the handful of rebels who had remained with him (most had stayed in the Labor Party, and those who followed him soon left) decided to put their case to the electorate in a by-election held in the Lancashire textile town of Ashton. The New Party received about 4,000 votes, not enough to win, but sufficient to keep the Labor Party's candidate from winning and to let the Conservative in. Outside the Ashton Town Hall, on election night, the working class crowd, who were mostly Labor supporters, was (as John Strachey later wrote in *The Menace of Fascism,* London: 1933), "violently hostile to Mosley and the New Party. It roared at him and, as he stood facing it, he said to me: 'That is the crowd that has prevented anyone doing anything in England since the war.' At that moment British Fascism was born."

Against the conservatism of professed social-democrats, against the obtuseness of the popular majority, only forcible means could triumph. The country should be saved even against its thoughtless inertia by men who knew what measures were needed for its good. On August 1, 1927, Mosley had declared that "the greatest danger to peace in Europe is the growth of Fascist power in Italy." In January 1932, he visited Rome, where he had long interviews with Mussolini and with the Secretary of the Fascist Party, Starace. In August 1932, Mosley assumed sole leadership in the New Party and, a few weeks later, concomitant with the publication of *The Greater Britain* (*see Reading No. 5A*), the New Party became the British Union of Fascists.

The purpose of the B.U.F. was clear: to carry out the ideas expressed in the Manifesto and then developed in *The Greater Britain,* ideas which soft, corrupted democracy had spurned. The Corporate State that the B.U.F. envisaged would "convert the existing chaotic survival of *laissez-faire* liberalism into a planned economy serving the needs of the State as a whole." The state envisaged would be authoritarian, and based on Mosley's blackshirts, who claimed to be essentially a national movement whose policy was contained in two words: "Britain First."

Many of Mosley's early followers came from the Labor Party, from Communism, and from Labor's radical wing —the Independent Labor Party (I.L.P.). When his black-shirts first appeared, they had been trained by a Jewish boxing champion, Kid Lewis, whom British Fascism's most objective historian, Colin Cross, describes as "a man of lively social conscience and simple outlook, who had volunteered to act as Mosley's personal bodyguard." One of the leading organizers of the B.U.F., Tommy Moran, an ex-miner, had resigned from the secretaryship of a Labor Party office to join in 1933. With membership of this kind, one would expect little tenderness for conservatism or private capital. "You will see the Tory monument on the banks of the Clyde, on Tyneside, in derelict Lancashire, in the Midlands, in the vast agricultural communities now stirring in revolt," wrote one of the editors of the party newspaper, himself a former member of the I.L.P. "These are the fruits of Toryism, and if this is the measure of their efficiency, then the sooner Britain is rid of them, the better for Britain. . . ."

There was no more sympathy for the established order in Mosley's own statements. Before 10,000 Fascists assembled in London's Albert Hall in April 1934, he made his position clear: "The present system, by its whole structure and methods, makes action impossible; more than that, it produces a type of man to whom action and decision are impossible, even if he had the power. We seek to establish a new ideal of public service, and a new system of authority which rests on merit." What this ideal should be became more obvious when the movement was reorganized in 1936 and changed its name from the British Union of Fascists to the British Union of Fascists and National Socialists. Something of a mouthful, the new title was rarely used in full and soon gave way to the British Union. At the same time "Fascist" and "Fascism" were used less and less, being replaced by "National Socialism." One of the favorite slogans of B.U.F.N.S. propaganda was: "If you love your country, you are a National, if you love her people you are a Socialist—Be a National Socialist."

In the spirit of the 1930 Manifesto, this National Socialism was held to be "a practical socialism," combining the best of Right and Left, and reviving the best of Robert Owen's Plan of 1816 and Hyndman's Merrie England. What such an assertion forgot was the strong tincture of Nazi anti-Semitism which would become one of the most distinctive features of the Mosleyites.

The Doom of Violence. How did a movement born of well-founded reformist impatience among bona fide Socialists, in a country that had no anti-Semitic tradition or cause for one, degenerate into the foul-mouthed, brawling hooliganism which marked so much of its career? The answer seems to be manifold: violence itself was an intrinsic part of the attitude Mosley had adopted, of his contempt for the moderates that he had left behind and for the crowds which, unable to convince, he meant to tame and conquer. When Mosley became a Fascist, he adopted Fascist methods: he would beat his opponents out of the way; he would impress the timid with his force; he would attract the simple· with uniforms and prestige; he would instill his followers with a sense of power and his enemies with fear by triumphal marches. And, to some extent, this worked.

But the British middle class was not ruined, not in terror of social revolution, not harassed or excited enough to join his ranks in sufficient numbers. Most respectable people were shocked by Fascist hooliganism, even when they might have accepted its authoritarian ideas. And the workers were solidly organized in great Trade Unions, with a doctrine which, part-Socialist, part-Chapel, seemed to suit their needs. The Communist Party had made little progress in England, far from enough progress to scare the tenants of the *status quo,* and British Fascism had to look elsewhere. Cranky recruits from the decaying upper middle classes, retired soldiers, impoverished gentlewomen, tweedy gentry, clerks who aspired to higher positions, were not enough. The movement needed a popular following not to be found among organized labor. It sought this among the *Lumpenproletariat:* roughs, toughs, hooligans, odd laborers out on a lark, youths from good families, "nice boys" from private schools whom the excitement attracted almost like a sport.

How could Mosley call to these people? Not with the charms of a doubtful present comfort or an imaginary golden age: conservatism or reaction were not in his line. Nor with the consistent Socialist doctrines that would shock some, mean little to others, and which he had in any case abandoned. Revolutionary language was called for, but within limits comprehensible to such a public: something both accessible and striking. An enemy was needed on whom hostility and violence could be focused, a bellows for enthusiasm: not the upper classes, for he had cousins there and benefited from sympathies among them; not the bourgeoisie, for the term was not much in vogue in England —and in the middle class he sought adherents too; and certainly not the workers. There remained the aliens and, while in England Jews are not very obviously alien, they were, nevertheless, the only ones who would do. They would even do well: for many of Mosley's *Lumpenproletarians* came from London's East End, a quarter where there were many Jews against whom one could whip up hostility—or try. And such attempts would benefit from the reverberations which Nazi anti-Semitism was causing throughout Europe so that, if he did nothing else, it may be said that Mosley managed to awaken anti-Semitism in a country where it had never been a public issue.

Except for this distasteful success, Mosley achieved nothing. He held mammoth meetings at which his opponents were brutally beaten up; he organized marches which generally ended in pitched battles, and the Fascist stalwarts often escaped their despised enemies only under police protection. This last became less discriminating than had been its wont when, under heavy public pressure, the government at last banned the wearing of uniforms and deprived the Fascists of their distinctive shirts. Blackshirted or not, they continued to march until the eve of the war, during which time those leaders who did not escape to Germany were interned under Defense Regulations, and fussed about by old-fashioned defenders of the British liberties they had meant to suppress.

This failure, much more striking than those of other movements of the time, had its reasons. The B.U.F. represented nothing: the interests of capital were guarded by the Conservatives, those of labor by the unions. Neither did well, but neither knew or caused sufficient distress for a recourse to really drastic means. Many of the measures which the Manifesto had called for were undertaken by Conservative or National Union governments after 1932 and 1934; many more would be adopted during the period of the war. Mosley's Manifesto had been ahead of its time: that was all. But Mosley, the man, was ruined by his colos-

sal vanity, his readiness to despise those who would not
have him, his indiscriminate choice of associates, his opportunistic tendency to adopt whatever means seemed likely
to advance his personal ambitions—ambitions out of all
proportion to his capacity. All this could have meant success under other circumstances, in another country; in England it meant only notoriety and, later on, discredit.

— 11 —

SPAIN

Inertia and Reaction. The lag of Spain's political and
economic development behind that of the rest of Europe
meant that familiar problems would arise in the peninsula
later and in a different guise than elsewhere in the West.
The First World War was followed by bitter social struggles,
and most Spaniards agreed that fundamental reforms were
needed to haul the country into the 20th century. Instead
of reforms, however, the country got Primo de Rivera,
whose old-fashioned military dictatorship (1923-1930) kept
things jogging along in a conservative vein.

Authoritarian, patriotic, and anti-parliamentary, Primo
de Rivera was a great admirer of Mussolini. But his power
was not as solidly established as that of the Italian dictator;
it lacked the basic support of a disciplined party and also
the Fascist's unscrupulous organization of power. The end
of the twenties found the country bankrupt, the reserves
built up during the years of wartime neutrality spent, and
the goodwill that the dictator enjoyed among the aristocracy, the army, and the upper classes, ebbing fast. At the
beginning of 1930, Primo de Rivera resigned, and the
dissatisfaction he had stifled while in power rose up to
engulf the throne. In spite of having discarded his dictator,
the King's situation became more difficult. Municipal elec-

tions held in April 1931 returned a majority of Republicans and showed that the discredit of the dictatorial years reflected on the monarchy itself. Within a few days, Alfonso XIII left the country (although he did not abdicate the throne), and the Republic was proclaimed in Madrid.

The new Republic, which took over in the thick of a world depression, was from the first beset by serious difficulties: autonomist tendencies, especially in Catalonia; Catholic opposition to a regime which separated Church and State, and secularized the latter; hostility of an Army leadership, inflated in numbers and in self-importance, resenting policies that cut down both its credits and its size. A country whose new Constitution and representative institutions needed running in, would find it hard to cope with its most pressing problems, particularly unemployment, the violence of long-suppressed extremist parties, and the burning issue of land reform. A measure of land distribution was voted but was slow to be put into application. The peasants occupied the lands and had to be driven off by the forces of a regime they thought would free them. Meanwhile the activities of Communists, Socialists, Anarchists, and of the separatists in the Basque provinces and Catalonia threatened the unity and stability of the land.

National Syndicalism. It was during this period that a number of small, extremist nationalist movements appeared which would provide the theoretical and organizational groundwork of Spanish Fascism. One of these groups expressed its views in the pages of an obscure Madrid weekly, *La Conquista del Estado* (The Conquest of the State), which had begun publication only a few weeks before the monarchy's collapse. Its editor, Ramiro Ledesma Ramos, son of a village schoolteacher, worked in the post office. One of Spain's many poor university graduates, condemned to a threadbare existence in grubby clerical employment, Ledesma Ramos was fascinated by the German philosophy he had picked up at school. Despising demagogic Nationalists as reactionaries, he tried to reconcile the German influence with a radical point of view that would be neither liberal nor Marxist. Ledesma Ramos liked neither the Church nor the middle classes—both were too backward, cosmopolitan, and selfish for his taste. He wanted a national workers' movement, which would adapt anarcho-

syndicalism—the only native radical tradition of the country—to Spanish needs in a system which he called National
Syndicalism.

What the small group of Ledesma's followers (all students or university graduates in their early twenties) had
in common with anarcho-syndicalists was less ideas than a
mood, a common hostility towards capital which they
claimed prevented any solidarity of interests between capitalists and wage earners, a common hostility, too, to Parliament and to the institutions of the existing society. Being
Spanish, they could agree with Bakunin's extreme statement that personal liberty and dignity consists of obeying
no other man and acting solely according to one's own
convictions. Being poor and restless, they could endorse
his advice that "the present generation must indiscrimi-
nately and blindly destroy everything that exists." * Unlike
the anarchists, however, they were not federalist and, above
all, far from anti-state. They liked neither the Right, which
they considered much too backward, nor the Left, which
they found far too doctrinaire; to remedy Spain's stagna-
tion and reconquer for her a worthy international position,
they saw no other instrument than that of a reinvigorated
state.

The program they announced in the first number of
La Conquista envisaged a new state which would be "constructive" and "creative," ready to "supplant individuals
and groups"; "the ultimate sovereignty will reside in it and
only in it." It was not certain quite how such an overween-
ing power would reconcile itself with a syndicalist economy
where the necessities of production would be owned in
common by the workers through labor groups and, perhaps,
free communes. But a unitary statism took precedence over
syndicalist ideals: in the State they planned, the "syn-
dication of economic forces will be obligatory, and in
each instance bound to the highest ends of the State. The
State will discipline and will guarantee production at all
times. . . ." The fierce individualism of the anarchists was
abandoned for a familiar elitism: "Our primary goal is
revolutionary efficiency. Therefore we do not seek votes,
but audacious and valiant minorities. . . ."

* This and other quotations are taken from S. Payne, *Falange*
    (Stanford: 1961), pp. 13, 31-32, 82, 266. By permission
    of Stanford University Press.

In effect, though he objected to the anarcho-syndicalists' lack of national sense, Ledesma Ramos liked their freedom from international connections and from bourgeois individualism. But the writers of *La Conquista* were trying to elaborate an ideology of their own, Nationalistic, Statist, imperialistically concerned with Spanish grandeur, calling for the expropriation of the great estates and the syndicalization of the masses. Although *La Conquista* soon disappeared because of lack of funds, its ideas would spread in university and right-wing circles and would coalesce with those of another small group founded about the same time as that of Ledesma Ramos's by the son of a peasant from Castile, Onesimo Redondo.

During the late twenties, while attending a Catholic German school, Redondo had become acquainted with German National Socialism. As much of a Spanish nationalist as Ledesma, he approached the problem of Spanish revival from another pole: Ledesma came from the Left, Redondo came from the Right. His doctrine combined ideas borrowed from the Nazis with a fervent "Spanish" Catholicism—intolerant, chivalric, but also "Social." His review, *Liberty,* published in Valladolid, called for "a movement steeped in true Spanish frenzy, launched by the young, and dedicated to combatting at every turn not only the uncontrolled wave of materialism, but also the irresponsible hypocrisy of the bourgeoisie."

Although Ledesma's was radical and Redondo's was religious, both movements were weak, short of funds, violent, nationalistic, anti-bourgeois and anti-Marxist. They would soon unite in the *Juntas de Ofensiva Nacional Sindicalistas* (Committees of National Syndicalist Offensive), or JONS, of which the yoked arrows of Ferdinand and Isabella were the emblem. And just as the Nazis and Rexists would take over the red banners of their enemies, the JONS adopted as their colors the red and black of Spanish Anarchism.

José Antonio. The JONS were fated to slumber until a man of stature took their leadership: José Antonio Primo de Rivera (1903-1936). José Antonio, son of the late dictator, had little sympathy for aristocrats and property-owning classes to which he himself belonged by right of birth, because he knew they had made the most of his father's dictatorship only to let him down when he could be of no more use. His entry into politics, however, was made—and very naturally—as candidate of the Right and champion of his father's memory. The first years of the Republic would give him food for thought and, by 1933, his earlier views had been modified towards an authoritarian Nationalism in which social reform played an important part. There was little definition of just what such reform might be (apart from distribution of the land), but an abstract idealistic vision, which by now we know as typical of Fascist romanticism (*see Reading No. 6A*):

> Fascism was born to inspire a faith not of the Right (which at bottom aspires to conserve everything, even injustice) or of the Left (which at bottom aspires to destroy everything, even goodness), but a collective, integral, national faith. . . .
>
> A fascist state is not created by the triumph of either the strongest or the most numerous party—which is not the right one for being the most numerous, although a stupid suffrage may say otherwise—but by the triumph of a principle of order common to all, the constant national sentiment, of which the state is the organ. . . .
>
> If anything truly deserves to be called workers' state, it is the fascist state. Therefore, in the fascist state—and the workers will come to realize this, no matter what—the workers' syndicates are directly elevated to the dignity of organs of the state. . . . One achieves true human dignity only when one serves. Only he is great who subjects himself to taking part in the achievement of a great task.

Falange. As a commentator pointed out, one had only to replace "Fascist" by "Socialist" to have a great many Marxists accepting such ideas. But José Antonio was no Marxist, as he proved by getting himself elected to the Cortes on a right-wing list in the elections of 1933. Except for a group of students enthused by his romantic rhetoric, the political movement he launched that same year, the *Falange Española,* was joined mostly by conservatives who followed him because he was his father's son.

Whatever its program, no extreme right party was likely to flourish once the moderate conservatives won the elections of 1933. The moderate public and the great money interests had no particular inclination towards violent action or authoritarian doctrines, provided they could protect their interests by legal means within the framework of exist-

ing institutions. It was during these doldrums, in 1934, that
Falange Española merged with JONS, José Antonio becoming the united movement's leader. Ledesma largely
drafted the new Falange's program, which served to break
the last connections with the conservative Right, already
alienated by a feeling that the Falangists meant what they
said when they called for social justice, and that a national-
syndicalist regime would not be much better than the
Socialism they feared.

While Falangist students exchanged blows and shots
with militants of the Left, and lent a ready hand in crush-
ing the miners' revolt in the Asturias, José Antonio established his hold on the movement, its syndicalist organizations, its sections of armed terrorists, excluding one after
the other, Ledesma Ramos and Onesimo Redondo, who
would lose their lives soon after, in the civil war. The
doctrine he developed stressed the need for a revolutionary elite to carry out Spain's social and economic revolution, but an elite that would be self-selected by work and
faith, and not by birth or education. No enthusiastic admirer of Mussolini or of Hitler, he stressed that the Falange
was not a Fascist movement, and that it had a *Spanish*
doctrine of its own. In any case, as Stanley Payne remarks,
the mass of Falangists had little or no idea of ideology:
"All they knew of their program was that it was radical,
ultranationalist, and stood for social reform. They knew
that the party planned some sort of new economic order
because José Antonio told them so, but they had only
vague ideas about the nature of that order. Their enemies
were the Left, the Center, and the Right; they hated the
Left and the separatists most of all. . . ." Anti-separatism
for Falangists was an article of faith: only unity could
make the country strong. Autonomy for Catalonia would
mean decay for Spain. And separatism itself was often
identified with policies of the Left.

But all this brought little support to the Falange. In the
elections of 1936, opposed both by the Left and Right,
José Antonio lost his seat, no other Falange candidate won
one, and the party as a whole polled only just over 40,000
votes throughout the country. The victors in the election
were the Popular Front, a coalition of left-wing parties
from Communists to the center-left, and José Antonio's

first reaction was to instruct his district leaders to avoid
identification with the defeated Right. What the Falange
hoped was that the revolutionary aspirations of the Left
might now be canalized by their nationalist influence. They
even tried to patch up an alliance with the more nationalist-
minded among the Socialists. But these plans came to nothing, and the movement slipped back into the right-wing fold.

Eager for the fruits of victory, some anarchists and
socialists were taking things into their own hands, attacking property—particularly that of churches. This only confirmed conservative fears of a red terror they had no intention of accepting. As violence increased, political parties
set up their own militias and, for a little while, funds flowed
more freely into Falangist coffers—the movement's idealism
and aggressiveness suggesting its potential role in the war
of terrorism and counter-terrorism that was beginning to
break out. Leftist militiamen looked on the Falange as a
dangerous enemy, while recruits from the Right came to
swell the Falange's armed bands. By March 1936, as murder and counter-murder swept the streets, the *Falange Española* was outlawed for being "an anticonstitutional party"
and most of its leaders thrown into jail. The party had to
go underground, while murders and arrests continued at an
increasing rate.

The Rising and the Fall. During this time a number of
army leaders were planning the rising which that summer
led to civil war. From jail, José Antonio was involved in
the discussions and the planning, as was the provincial
leadership of the now-underground Falange; but the generals and the colonels were determined to keep control of
any insurrection, while José Antonio did not trust even
their will to rise. When the rebellion came (17-18 July,
1936), the Falangists played their part, first as independent
civilian auxiliaries to rebel army units, then in uniform. The
party now became the leading nationalist political formation, its ranks swelled not only by nationalist enthusiasts,
but by syndicalists and "leftists" who sought refuge from
the persecutions of the Right.

But though it waxed in numbers, the movement had been
decapitated. José Antonio and several other leaders would
die or rot in the Republic's prisons; the survivors would
be brought to heel by the army leaders. Two principal

political organizations existed in nationalist territory: the
Falange, and the deeply Catholic, traditionalist followers of
a Bourbon pretender to the throne—the Carlists, with their
military formations called *Requetés*. In 1937, these were
fused by Franco's fiat in an artificial and theoretically
absurd formation which bore the name *Falange Española
Tradicionalista y de las JONS*—clearly, as Franco put it in
the decree that launched it, "a movement more than a
program," a movement under the personal leadership of
Franco himself.

In Italy and Germany, the party had conquered the
state: in Spain, the generals who conquered the state conquered the party too and turned it into a kind of zombie
whose principal task would be to harness the workers to
the chariot of their authoritarian rule. The old Falange
leaders who survived were arrested, many were condemned
to death and, though not executed, imprisoned, banished,
or forced to take refuge abroad. Falange principles would
be proclaimed "the source of inspiration and the law of
the Spanish State"; but the conservatism of Franco and
the traditionalism of Carlist elements would give the party
a very different coloring from that of 1934. It would fulfill
its role as the party of the state—the docile, if sometimes
resentful, instrument of Franco.

In later years, young rebel groups would form within
and outside its ranks, resentful of the new regime's stodgy
conservatism and hoping to reaffirm the original national-
syndicalist ideas that the Caudillo had thrown overboard.
Along with the Falange, Franco's regime kept much of the
tone of José Antonio's speeches, but little of its spirit, if
at all. Stanley Payne concludes that by 1959 *"falangismo,*
as an organized living force, was entirely dead." Spain
looked to Marxism or to the Church, with its wide diversity
of orientations; but, though the Falange lived on, hardly
to the Falange.

The true Falangists have moved to other parties. Thus,
in 1962, Dionisio Ridruejo, who many years ago composed
the Falange's hymn and fought in Russia in the Spanish
"Blue Division," and who is now a leader of *Accion Demo-
cratica,* was asked why, after having helped to found the
Falange, he has become one of the regime's most determined opponents. "It is very simple," answered Ridruejo:

"When the civil war began, I was 23 years old and I believed in national revolution. Once victory had been won, I realized that I had helped a hardened oligarchy into power. So I began to fight it."

— 12 —

BELGIUM

Degrelle. The history of Rex, and of its living embodiment Léon Degrelle, is typical of a Fascist movement in a western democracy: a country whose problems were in no way dramatic and whose people, solid and often stolid, inclined neither to excesses nor to histrionics.

Léon Degrelle was born in 1906, at Bouillon in the Ardennes, Shakespeare's forest of Arden, close to the French border. He came from a family which, as a Belgian bishop maliciously expressed it, produced Jesuits from father to son. Léon's father was born near Maubeuge, in northern France, and his mother's family came from German-speaking Moselle; but the Degrelles were an old clan, widespread throughout the lowland countries that had once been part of a greater Burgundy and which Degrelle would one day try to reintegrate.

The boy soon discovered the ideas of the French monarchist and reactionary *Action Française*—a very popular movement in the Belgium of the early twenties, particularly among the Jesuits and other teaching orders in Catholic schools. From the *Action Française* newspaper and its polemicist, Léon Daudet, Degrelle drew the verve and the biting, droll, and brilliant style of his own polemics. But it was Charles Maurras who affected him most. From him, Degrelle learned to despise democracy, the stupidity of masses and of majority rule, the irresponsibility and corruption of parliamentary assemblies. Maurras's arguments convinced him that order, competence, continuity, and responsibility—capped by one keystone, monarchy—were the only foundation on which to build a viable state. Though by the age of 21 he had broken loose from the *Action Française*, these ideas were to stay with him and to provide the basis of Rex's doctrine.

The flamboyant movement of the middle thirties had its origins in a small Catholic publishing firm, Christus-Rex, launched under the auspices of the A.C.J.B. (Catholic Association of Belgian Youth) whose management Degrelle undertook in 1930. From his tiny offices in the Louvain headquarters of the A.C.J.B., Degrelle showered Belgium with pamphlets, posters, and periodicals destined "to renovate Christian life." It is important to remember that Degrelle always remained a keen practicing Catholic, and that his first motives were those of many other young men who set out to assert high-minded principles (and themselves, of course) in the junk yard of fudge and compromise where the older generation seems to be contented. Catholic action, apostolic spirit, the rejuvenation of Catholicism and thus of Belgium, sound like admirable aspirations—at least for Catholics. Such sentiments, however, only too often end in condemnation, compromise, or abandon. At any rate, they are bound to seek political expression sooner or later.

Rex. This is what happened with the young men of Christus-Rex. Their ideals sought a political expression. But politics of an active and reformist kind were difficult in a country where political differences had become particularly shallow, and no political party (except that of the Flemish Nationalists who demanded regional autonomy) seemed to have a well-defined policy. Ever since 1914, Belgium had been ruled by coalitions—Catholic, Liberal and Socialist, or Socialist-Catholic—before whose pragmatic convenience ideologies had withered away. Their doctrines increasingly forgotten, the parties had traded whatever enthusiasm they might have once had for practical economic and administrative concerns. Young Belgian intellectuals, eager for an idea, found only pragmatic materialism. Against this background of political meaninglessness, many welcomed Rex's attempt to revive the feeling that meaningful action was possible, and Rexist insistence that Rex was a *movement*—a living part of life. (*See Reading No. 7A.*) Before it did anything else, this insistence on movement alone ("Rex is not a party and does not want to be one. . . . It is an enormous sentimental movement. Rex is a movement, that is an active force, carrying a current of ideas. . . .") gave both followers and leaders a sense of activity and, almost, a sense of achievement.

But such a feeling had to be reinforced by action. Degrelle and his friends, few of them over 25, had sought at first to express themselves through the existing Catholic party. They had found it sclerotic, deeply committed to the existing system, its integrity corrupted by the "banksters," and its leaders involved in the very frauds and swindles Rex wanted to sweep away. Degrelle's denunciations of corrupt politicians, particularly his attack on the President of the Catholic Party and Minister of State, Segers, forced him to break with the A.C.J.B. It was at this time that Rex adopted the broom as its most characteristic device, and sent troops of young men to sweep the pavement outside the headquarters of various parties, especially the Catholic party, and outside the Parliament building. In late 1935, having antagonized practically every organized political force in the country, Rex stood alone, its chief and almost its only assets being the extraordinary dynamism of Léon Degrelle, a devoted organizational network covering the country on a shoestring, and the drab flabbiness of the men it opposed.

In a country where political meetings hardly ever drew more than a few hundred people, thousands came—and paid admission—to hear Degrelle. They packed meetings which Rex always staged with impressive displays of banners, bands, searchlights, and massed groups of guards. To a public bored by the petty issues of local politics and disinclined to believe that even these could be coped with by the ruling cliques, the Rexist speakers held another language, more elevating, more inspiring. The world, they said, was rotten with selfishness and greed. Only those could save it who were willing to sacrifice themselves every day, transcend the preoccupations of their little lives in order to fulfill a higher, grander goal. To a largely bourgeois public, Rex spoke in violently anti-bourgeois tones, even its anti-Communism becoming an excuse to attack the conservative enemies not only of Communism but of the country's welfare:

> We are not the sort to exploit the funk of frightened bourgeois by telling them that Communism and revolution are one. We are those who, having nothing to lose and everything to win, have decided to replace the decaying liberal regime with a new regime and to create a world in which a man can truly live. We can expect nothing from the present regime against which we are in open insurrection. We would not write a line, we would not say a word, we would not shed a drop of our blood, to defend it; and if it was a question of consolidating it, let us tell you frankly, at the risk of scandalizing the weak, that we would just as soon have a Communist regime.

Rexist opposition to Communism itself was based on the belief that Marxism was a left-over of decaying liberalism. To the capitalism of the "banksters," Communism substituted a state capitalism just as one-sided and oppressive. In every other way, argued José Streel (who would be shot at the liberation), the Communists merely developed the themes of the existing regime: "Communism is not revolution against established disorder, but simply the extension of this disorder and the exasperation of its essential vices." And Degrelle: "To break the neck of Communism will get us nowhere if we do not also break the neck of the social selfishness that gave it birth."

"It was by calling for devotion, by exalting renunciation, abnegation, purity, labor, the will to serve," wrote *La Nation Belge,* a none too friendly Brussels daily, "that Degrelle wrung the loudest applause from the crowd of average Belgians, tradesmen, workers, clerks, petty bourgeois. Our fathers would have been amazed to see this. . . ." (*See Reading No. 7B.*) Rival party politicians also were amazed.

Success. The movement's publications supported its propaganda: the weekly *Rex* appeared in three editions: French for the Walloons, Flemish, and German for the population of Eupen and Malmédy (formerly German territory), annexed in 1918. A daily, *Pays réel* (a title of Maurassian inspiration, opposing the *real* nation to its merely *legal,* formal institutions), printed over 200,000 copies on weekdays and one million on Sundays. The second half of 1936 also saw the foundation of a Flemish-language daily, *Die Nieuwe Staat,* for Rex wanted to reconcile the country's bitterly antagonistic linguistic groups. All this cost money, and Rex could not look for support from the financial interests it lambasted daily. After its electoral success, business interests would run to help, and one great industrialist alone would send two million francs (about $1,500,000 today) to cover 120,000 subscriptions to *Pays réel;* but at first reasonable people both feared and discounted the possibility of such successes. Rex's funds came from the admission fees to its meetings (none of which were free) and from Italian subsidies made available by Mussolini.

The affinities between Degrelle's ideas and Mussolini's were close: the same national-activist appeal, the same slogans of national revival, the same popular following in strongly Catholic countries; but the personal sympathy between the two men was even greater. Mussolini, who thought that Degrelle resembled him, intervened several times to smooth the younger man's path, allowing him to use the Italian radio when the Belgian government refused him time that other political formations had been allowed on the national broadcasting system, and probably preventing a papal condemnation of Rex. Degrelle, for his part, appreciated support from a regime he admired but which was far enough away not to have any particular interests in Belgium. Hitler, he admired, but somewhat distrusted. Mussolini, he could afford to trust; he certainly could not have afforded to do without him.

But who were those who backed Rex in Belgium? It would seem they were mainly the youth and the petty bourgeoisie of a Catholic country, who were hit by the depression, disgusted by the impotence of the ruling parties and even more by the squalid corruption that Rex's campaigns revealed. Working-class support, eagerly sought, was thinner; but Degrelle's persistence and his courage in confronting the working-class public of the industrial and mining regions won him some adherents, and a great factory center like Charleroi elected a Rexist in 1936. It was not the only town to do so: Verviers elected two Rexist deputies, Liège three deputies and two senators—one of them a sometime-Socialist syndicalist. Altogether, in the elections of May

1936, 21 Rexist deputies (out of 202) and 12 senators were returned to Parliament.

In the wake of the elections (and inspired by similar events in France) great strikes broke out, with their inevitable train of violence and grief. Degrelle's more respectable electors were shocked when, contrary to all expectations, their champion took the strikers' side, supporting their demands for a 40-hour week and instructing the Rexist group to vote in their favor, setting up soup kitchens and evacuation centers for miners' children, arguing that one must not fall into the trap of opposing just demands merely because of Communist spokesmanship or Communist-fomented violence. The conservative public waxed indignant, but Degrelle carried on. It was essential that the Communists be dislodged from their privileged position as defenders of the people: "Without the people, a party is nothing. The bourgeois comes and goes, he gives himself when all goes well and wets his trousers when things start to go badly. Then he takes off, with a wet behind. The real tough ones, the ones that hold good through thick and thin, because their attachment is not subordinated to the protection of material goods, are the people. Either you have the people with you, or you have nothing with you."

All this was disturbing. And when, in October 1936, Degrelle concluded a pact with the Flemish Nationalists, whom most Walloons considered deeply subversive, and recognized their federalist demands, fear spread that Rex might attempt a *coup d'état*. Fear, and in some quarters hope: for important elements of the army, leading conservative politicians, and perhaps the king himself, would not have minded seeing such a coup succeed. Degrelle, however, was a legalist, and the revolution he proposed, at least at that particular time, was not to involve any but legal means. The diversity and inexperience of Rexist deputies made them useless for any task but that of disrupting Parliamentary sittings, but the movement's following was growing—even in popular quarters—and in January 1937, Degrelle filled the Palais des Sports, Brussels' Madison Square Garden, night after night for a week.

Failure. Confident that in fresh elections Rex was bound to win at least a controlling minority of seats, Degrelle now tried to force the moderate leftist government

of Premier Van Zeeland to dissolve Parliament and proceed to new elections. In February 1937, he faced Van
Zeeland in a by-election in Brussels, designed to achieve
that very end, but he lost. All the forces of conservatism
had joined against him, from the Communist advocates of
a moderate Popular Front to the Catholics, admonished by
the Belgian primate, Cardinal Van Rooey, that it would be
a sin even to abstain. Against Van Zeeland's 275,000,
Degrelle got only 69,000 votes.

Rex seemed to have been a flash in the pan. In the
elections of 1939, although Degrelle himself was returned
in Brussels with the greatest majority of any deputy, the
Rexist group in Parliament had been reduced from 21 to 4.
The Liberals and the Catholics were recapturing the voters
they had lost. Above all, Degrelle's insistent pacifism and
neutralism, in the wake of Munich and on the eve of im-
pending war, was turning Belgian patriots against him, some
of them even within Rex itself. Only the German occupation (1940-1944) would bring Rex into its own again.

Occupation and Collaboration. In June 1940 Henri de
Man, leader of Belgian Labor, dissolved his party and
advised his followers: "War has brought the downfall of
the parliamentary regime and of capitalist plutocracy in
the so-called democracies. For the working classes and for
Socialism, this collapse of a decrepit world, far from being
a disaster, comes as a liberation." Nazi friends of Degrelle
and of de Man, in the Socialist and internationalist circles
connected with Otto Abetz, tried to give Belgium a government headed by the two men, but their scheme failed before
opposition from more conservative quarters. So, at the outbreak of the German war in Russia (1941), Degrelle joined
the Legion of Walloon volunteers which Rex helped the
Germans raise for the Eastern front.

Some of the Legion's most enthusiastic volunteers seem
to have come from the ranks of ex-Communists (several
hundred of whom followed Degrelle to Russia) and from
the Socialist combat organization, *Jeunes gardes socialistes,*
which had been Rex's fiercest foes before the war. "There
were no fiercer enemies of Fascism than these rugged men,"
recalled Degrelle. "But, when you came down to it, no one
was better prepared for the violence of the regimes they
liked to brand with infamy. . . . This Socialist youth had

ideals. It burned to join us in creating a powerful socialism."
A German victory would fulfill their dreams of international unity and of social revolution. "Europe," Degrelle
argued, "must be one, in order to carry out the National
Socialist revolution under the aegis of the SS."

But, though he may have been a "European," Degrelle
remained a Belgian nationalist. His dreams revived the
childhood memories of a greater Burgundy and, behind it,
Lotharingia—a realm in which Belgians would play the
leading role. In Germany's new Europe a people's role and
rank would depend on the regard the Nazis had for it.
Military valor was the way to Hitler's favor; distinction in
battle the only means to win German respect. And, in a
sense, his calculation was correct: enlisted as a simple
soldier, commissioned in the field and five times wounded,
at the war's end Degrelle achieved the rank of a Division
Commander. He was decorated for his bravery with the
highest German order, the Knight's Cross of the Iron
Cross, by Hitler himself. Degrelle had won the confidence
and the respect of the Führer and of his aides, who destined
him to rule in Belgium, and perhaps also in a greater
Burgundy.

But such hard-won successes sank without trace, along
with the Führer's fortune. Of the original Walloon con-
tingent of 850, only three men survived; all told, after three
years' fighting, 2500 Walloons had left their bones on the
Eastern front and on the long way back. Degrelle himself
made his escape by a hair-raising flight from Norway to
Spain on VE night and there (or elsewhere) survives, turning out memoirs highly embarrassing to Belgian politicians,
a man whose dynamism and burning ambition twice raised
him very close to the power he coveted, only to dash him
down again.

FRANCE

Nationalism and Socialism. The first meeting of Socialist and nationalist in France seems to have occurred in the pages of *La Cocarde* (1894-1895). Its contributors who came from all extremes of the political horizon rejected class war in favor of class integration without, however, approving a capitalist and bourgeois order they all despised. It was this rejection of bourgeois order and bourgeois democracy that provided the basis of the next significant reconciliation of the two points of view, which took place first within the royalist movement of the *Action Française*, and then between some of its members and the syndicalist followers of Georges Sorel.

It is not generally appreciated that the *Action Française*, which never hid its reactionary views, had been before 1914 extremely interested in questions of social reform and in the possibility of attracting a working-class public it vigorously wooed with posters, with meetings, and with tracts. "We are nationalistic and consequently social," Maurras declared, for his critique of individualism and liberalism had led him to positions very similar to those of Socialists who were, like him, concerned with a public good superior to the private; like him, too, aware that a society whose members are left to themselves will tend towards anarchy and the tyranny of the strongest.

Where Charles Maurras differed from the Socialists was not in matters of social *concern*, but in matters of social *order*—denouncing their equalitarian ideas and the belief that authority stems from the mass. To him, authority was clearly established only by the natural hierarchy of competence and birth. This meant that Maurras opposed Socialist democracy, and Socialist internationalism as well. "There is opposition, contradiction, between equalitarian and international Marxism and the protection of nation and of fatherland," we read in his *Political and Critical Dictionary*. "But a socialism delivered of democratic and cosmopolitan elements can fit nationalism like a well-made glove fits a beautiful hand."

This hand-in-glove relationship would be tried and found wanting before the First World War, in the stormy courtship of Maurras and Georges Sorel. About 1907, Sorel had started to ease away from the syndicalist movement which he found too ready to compromise with bourgeois parties for some immediate gain. Within a few years the old theoretician had come to agree with the Italian, Benedetto Croce, that "socialism is dead," and to appreciate the potential public that the radical nationalists of the *Action Française* could offer. Projects were mooted for a review to be run jointly by nationalists and syndicalists, for which Sorel even drew up the draft of a manifesto: "This review addresses itself to reasonable men who have been sickened by the humanitarian bilge, by the fashions come to us from abroad. . . ." But the review fell through and it was not until 1911 that another National Socialist publication could appear, the *Independence,* whose steadiest contributor would be Sorel: a patriotic, nationalistic, anti-Semitic Sorel, who compared France's struggle against the Jews to America's struggle against the yellow peril and who flourished surrounded by Maurras's *Camelots du Roi.*

But the more intellectual among the *Camelots* could not be satisfied with Sorel's rather anarchic criticisms. They wanted to clear up the persistent confusion between liberty and disorder, and they wanted an opportunity for National Socialistic studies of economic problems. In answer to their demands, in December 1911, the *Cercle Proudhon* would hold its first meeting under the presidency of Charles Maurras. Long before Marx, Pierre-Joseph Proudhon (1809-1865) had denounced the spoliation of workers by capital and declared that "property is theft"—referring to the great accumulations of property which take, or profit from, the product of other people's labor without giving them a fair equivalent. But, unlike that of Marx, the revolution Proudhon advocated was meant to establish a society in which class reconciliation, the right of work for all, and each man's right to property and to his own way of life, would, as he put it, unite order and anarchy. In the *Cahiers du cercle Proudhon* disciples of Maurras, of Bergson, of

Sorel, all agreed that "democracy is the greatest error of the past century," the enemy of both culture and productivity. Democracy, with its individualistic, liberal chaos, was responsible for the exploitation of labor, as it was responsible for the destructive capitalism they all opposed. Against democracy, against parliamentarism and socialism, against the fat, self-satisfied bourgeois society then enjoying the tag-end of its security, the young men dreamed brave and violent dreams of social and moral reform on an authoritarian basis.

The war, which cut short their lives, also cut short their dreams. After the war, a weary public was bent on relaxation, the vested interests on a return to business as usual. Nationalism rode into power with the cohorts of militant conservatism, who looked forward to going back, vizualized victory in terms of Fourteenth of July parades extended to Alsace-Lorraine, and squabbled endlessly over issues which had been exhausted long before the war.

Valois. But the Fascist adventure in Italy revived memories of the *Cercle Proudhon,* and particularly inspired one of the *Cercle's* survivors, Georges Valois, a dynamic, self-taught economic thinker of great vanity, originality and talent. He had joined the *Action Française* in the belief that the royalist movement would help realize his plans for socio-economic reform on corporatist lines. To him, "Nationalism + Socialism = Fascism." His ideal was to persuade workers to act together, regardless of traditional labels and divisions which were irrelevant to their true interests. His great success in the middle twenties was the debauching of the Communist mayor of Périgueux, in central France, whom he persuaded that Communist activity could be carried out on the national plane, a point of view which led that gentleman out of Communist into Fascist ranks before returning him to obscurity and oblivion.

Valois himself left the *Action Française* in 1925, because he sought a more lively activity, both national and Socialist, than Maurras's movement could furnish after the war had drained it of its most social-minded members. Instead, with a group of veteran friends, he founded the *Faisceau* (the *Fascio* of Fighters and Producers by its full title), a French version of Mussolini's *fascios,* directly and unequivocally inspired by its transalpine forerunners. "Our aim," he would declare on November 11, 1925, "is conquest of the State in order to set up a new political, economic and social organization, and to bring about the revival of France. We shall achieve this conquest at the very moment when the parliamentary State, powerless to overcome its difficulties, will collapse or disappear."

Veterans flocked with enthusiasm into the ranks of the new organization. Disgruntled by the financial crisis of the times, disillusioned by a world very difficult for heroes to live in and in which no one asked their advice, dreaming of an orderly, comradely, and "pure" society, the cream of combat veterans donned the blue shirts of the *Faisceau* and marched in its parades. Communists came to join them, and also syndicalist leaders like Henri Loridan, who had made his name organizing the powerful textile unions in the north, and very bright young men like Philippe Lamour, who has since become one of France's great economic managers. For a moment, Parliament, banks and unions felt the touch of fear before the activities of this lively and active opposition. Then Raymond Poincaré re-established the franc and, by 1928, the Fascist threat disintegrated before the indifference of a reassured public. Valois himself vegetated through the thirties, moving ever further left, connected now with Socialist, now with Trotskyite circles, but ever a disciple of the ethical Socialism of his first love— Proudhon. The Germans would deport him to Bergen-Belsen, where he would die shortly before British troops liberated the camp.

Leagues of the Thirties. In 1933, a lesser companion of the defunct *Faisceau,* much decorated Marcel Bucard, founded the *Francistes*—whose Fascism was more self-consciously National Socialist. Recruited in the popular quarters of Paris, the Francists tempted militants away from both the Communist and the Socialist parties. Their numbers remained small (in 1935, they claimed some 30,000 members), but 40 or 50% of them seem to have come either from the unions or the working-class parties. Characteristically, in the spring of 1934, we find the party declining an invitation to join a nationalist coalition, denying that Francism could be considered a right-wing movement, and sneering at the idea that there could be anything in common between Francists and "conservatives and re-actionaries."

Dissolved in 1936 by the Popular Front government of Léon Blum, the movement was resurrected by the Germans after 1940. Arrested in the Tyrol, where he had sought to hide after following his German patrons in their rout, Bucard would be condemned and shot in 1946. To this brave, unintelligent man, Fascism—and Francism—drew both its elements and its spirit from the Left; because "being the opposite of Marxism, it is much nearer social-ism—understood in the sense of social justice—than it is to bourgeois conservatism which it holds in horror."

There was no shortage in the middle thirties of leagues and parties all of which professed that Nationalism was social and Socialism necessarily national, most of which would have endorsed the words of Jacques Debu-Bridel (sometime of the *Action Française* and later of the *Fais-ceau*, who became during the war a member of the National Council of the Resistance and after it a Senator of the Fourth Republic): "We are anti-capitalist because we are national and anti-Marxist. . . . Our doctrine has its roots in the soil of France. The very term national Socialism can be found in one of our dearest masters: Barrès."

Such movements should not be confused with the thirties' most successful league—the *Croix de Feu* (Fiery Cross or, later, French Social Party) of Colonel Count de la Rocque. De la Rocque is often mentioned as a Fascist leader, but he was no more than an upper-middle-class Poujade. Al-though as a soldier he distrusted liberalism, his calls for change echoed the hopes of the possessing classes. His views seem to have come from Samuel Smiles and from *Poor Richard's Almanack:* end of social insurance and of exces-sive unemployment relief, end of state interference and the sale of state monopolies to private enterprises, lower taxes, no more cheap lodgings "built without taste and full of suspect elements, fortresses of the Popular Front," end of an absurd educational policy that kept too many people from learning the virtues of manual labor at an early age.

Colonel de la Rocque was a respectable, law-abiding man, respectful of the established order at least to the extent of accepting government subsidies for his league. Most of his followers, like himself, were frightened by the Bolshevik menace, exasperated by economic straits and problems they could not begin to understand, anxious about the country's future and their own. But mass meetings and parades are not enough to make Fascists, and the *Croix de Feu* simply do not qualify as anything more than patriotic conservatives.

Doriot. Even without them, however, the crop is rich enough. In 1934, when he left the Communist Party asserting that "the great Marxist dream is bankrupt in Russia and elsewhere," Jacques Doriot (1898-1945) was one of the leaders of the Communist Party and master of one of its citadels—the industrial city of Saint Denis, near Paris. A veteran Marxist and a Communist deputy since 1924, he had early opposed Stalin's domination, insisted unsuccessfully on independence for the French Communist Party and also, before Moscow came around to it, on the importance of a left-wing alliance of workers, peasants and middle classes "which alone could oppose Fascism"—the prototype of the Popular Front formula which Moscow launched a year or two later. Censored by his party, Doriot persisted in his heresies, resigned the mayoralty of his city only to be re-elected triumphantly by a working-class electorate which also returned him to the chamber in spite of the Popular Front landslide of 1936. "A new formula must be found," Doriot declared. "All countries are not nationalistic, and internationalism is not only an error but a crime."

The P.P.F. (French Popular Party) which he now founded would, therefore, be "both national and social." As Drieu La Rochelle, one of the first to joint him, would explain, most of the leaders of the P.P.F. had at one time or another felt the attraction of Communism: "For years, Moscow was our great temptation—the temptation of our weakness. Since nothing was being done in France, we dreamed of all the things that were being done over there." The Fascist fascination could be much the same, and the P.P.F. would act, after 1936, as something of a catchall for social activists and authoritarians of every imaginable background: many Communists, of course, who had left the party in Doriot's wake; many syndicalists and sometime Socialist intellectuals, but also straightforward Fascists:

Victor Arrighi and Alfred Fabre-Luce from the Social National Party that Jean Hennessy, the cognac manufacturer,
had founded, followers of de la Rocque dissatisfied with
the moderation of the *Croix de Feu,* many young men who
had tried the possibilities of the *Action Française,* and a
host of others, not least questing intellectuals like Drieu
La Rochelle, the literary critic Ramon Fernandez, the
political scientist Maurice Duverger, and the philosopher
and publicist Bertrand de Jouvenel. As the latter admitted,
most P.P.F. men were inveterate joiners, league hopping
in search of salvation. They evidently thought to have found
it in the forceful man who proposed to tear away the
disfiguring mask of capitalism, reveal the true face of
France, and free it for its civilizing mission among the
backward nations.

As it turned out, the P.P.F. had to conduct its civilizing
mission under Nazi patronage. Until 1940, conditions in
France were never critical enough to shift a significant
portion of its people into the camp of violent change. The
workers for the most part were satisfied and, later, cowed;
the property-owning classes were not scared enough to go
beyond the moderate positions of the *Croix de Feu.* Under
the occupation, however, Doriot became one of the leaders
of collaboration, preaching a Fascist revolution and an
authoritarian regime (the masses which had scorned him
as they scorned Mosley were "weak, superficial, changing
and unreliable," and had to be ignored or dominated by
"the only great French revolutionary movement"—his
own). He would die on a German road, his car machine-
gunned by an allied aircraft, after having followed his masters out of liberated France.

Déat. A very different figure, Marcel Déat, had made
his way into politics by way of the University and had
made his mark in 1933 at that year's Socialist Congress
held in Paris. The speeches which he and his fellow-Social-
ist deputies, Adrien Marquet and Barthélémy Montagnon,
delivered on that occasion, argued in effect that the reigning plutocracy could be removed only by a revolution that
French Socialists as such had lost from view, a revolution
that was absolutely essential even if it turned out to be a
Fascist one.

Déat had already outlined these views two years before

in a perceptive book called *Socialist Perspectives* (1931), which had been published by none other than Georges Valois. The book insisted on the need for union with other opponents of the capitalist order, rather than purely socialist action on classic and isolated lines. Ten years later its author, whose pacifism had made him acceptable to the Germans, would found a party destined to carry out his ideas of 1931 and 1933. The *Rassemblement National Populaire* (National Popular Gathering) was founded in 1941 and died in 1944. During the first of these years it was colonized by the gangsters of Eugène Deloncle's pre-war terrorist Cagoule, revived by German warrant under the promising label of Social Revolutionary Movement (M.S.R.). Once rid of the M.S.R. gang, however, Déat drew his followers chiefly from the ranks of the academic and journalistic Left. This R.N.P., which included many syndicalists, stood for what Déat would call a modern Socialism: national, popular and authoritarian, anticapitalistic but not anti-Semitic, and anticlerical not on principle but only within the limits of immediate needs.

Like many intellectuals, Déat felt the need to reconcile apparently dissimilar and antagonistic phenomena and give his stand a respectable pedigree. He did this by arguing that the "German revolution" of National Socialism was a direct descendant of the ideas of 1789, and especially of the Jacobins of 1793 who had "engaged France upon the road of political totalitarianism, of a totalitarian conception of life and of the State," only to be defeated by the triumph of liberal capitalism. The argument is more interesting as a symptom than as an explanation, but Déat's movement provides an almost unique instance of a national-socialism that drew its inspiration and its cadres from the Left, where most of the others drew theirs either from the Right or from the sort of authoritarian opportunism we tend to associate with the "Fascist temperament."

Déat's own fate was odd: fleeing the Allies in 1945, he and his wife sought refuge in an Italian cloister. Hidden by the Catholic authorities, the couple, whom the world thought lost in some Alpine glacier, returned to their first profession—teaching—in Turin, where the sometime atheist would die in 1957 reconciled with the Church.

Fascist Fever. It is easy to understand why Léon Blum

should be appalled by the heretical prospects he glimpsed in 1933 in the words of men then still his fellow-Socialists: he could foresee their logical end in a National Socialist camp which had to be identified with Germany, Hitler, and death. But if they got there in the end, it must have been in good part because the conventional Socialist Party persisted in ignoring that reality of our time which Fascists accepted—more than accepted, felt in their bones: the need to *do* something and feel that something was being done, the will to motion for motion's sake, to action for action's sake, to revolution for revolution's sake.

Pierre Lassieur has expressed this sentiment very well in *The Story of a Man Condemned to Death* (Paris 1950), which is the fictionalized life of Robert Brasillach, the writer and poet whom execution (for collaboration, in 1944) has turned into one of the literary Right's most patented heroes. For Lassieur—as for Brasillach, whose boy scout enthusiasm at the Nuremberg rallies, in the extreme right press, in the Spanish holocaust, or in the vaster one that followed, remains the most striking thing about him—Fascism was a great romantic adventure. Not reason, but feeling, dragged him along the road of passionate action. Fascism offered the men of the Right what Communism offered to those of the Left: "the banners of revolution, the exaltation of the clan, the prestige of the leader, of his militias and his standards." People took Fascism for a policy; for many of those who thought about it (for most did not) it was much more a question of style—a way of being, of behaving, of reacting to the circumstances of life. For many of these enthusiasts, as for Brasillach himself, Fascism was never a doctrine, "but a great access of fever."

Much the same can be said, not in praise or in excuse (for feverish activity ends too often in disaster), but as a factual observation of many who adopted the Communist religion between the wars. And it may well be that the professional politicians who reinvented National Socialism in the France of the thirties—whether at the Socialist Congress of 1933 or soon thereafter at Saint Denis—while they were neither boy scouts nor irresponsible journalists driven by the impetus of their polemics, did also feel the touch of the prevailing fever. A Doriot, even a Déat, sensed the need for something: *not* more coherent, more logical, more theoretically perfect, but on the contrary, more incoherent, more attuned to the moment's complex demands. They sought a sort of revolutionary glamour, of revolutionary promise, that would not rest upon—and only upon—a body of doctrines cherished only by faithful doctrinaires and irrelevant to the tendencies of the public and the apparent needs of the moment.

— 14 —

CONCLUSION

Reaction. Twentieth-century Fascism is a by-product of disintegrating liberal democracy. Loss of hope in the possibilities of existing order and society, disgust with their corruption and ineffectiveness, above all the society's evident loss of confidence in itself, all these produce or spur a revolutionary mood in which the only issue lies in catastrophic action—but always with a strong social tinge: "I place my only hope in the continuation of socialist progress through fascisms," writes Drieu. And the editor of the French Fascist publication, the *Insurgent,* Jean-Pierre Maxence, would call insurgents of all parties to join "the front of united youth, for bread, for grandeur and for liberty, in immense disgust with capitalist democracy." From this angle, as from many others, Fascism looks much like the Jacobinism of our time.

There is no doubt that, at least in France, it was the failure, real or apparent, of the established order to stand up for itself and for its own—it was this failure that created and recruited the troops of a certain Fascist reaction. But the appearance of such movements may also be cited in evidence of the middle classes' determination to defend themselves—a mood which a Paris candidate expressed when she told her electors that she "remained violently moderate."

Movements of this sort can often be the pure expression of reaction. A social class or a body of men think their interests are threatened and organize to defend them. There is nothing "social" about such a reaction, it is hardly even a pretense. And since both reactionaries and Fascists exalt violence as part of their policy, the contradiction between the former, who want settled order and security, and the latter, who want to destroy the settled order, is lost from sight. But, while social reaction and social thoughtlessness have made their contribution to Fascism, we have seen that Fascist doctrines and the Fascist temper are far from reactionary in themselves.

Characteristics. The confusion is understandable. For though Fascist movements are revolutionary, they can only triumph in a situation which brings grist to their mill, by displacing people and resources from the camp of order into a no man's land where they will listen to their appeals. There is, indeed, a profound connection between this revolutionary character and what we know of Fascism's appeal to youth. In one sense, we recognize in all Fascist-type movements a rising of younger generations against the old who keep them from the manger. In 1933, Blum and Herriot in France were 61, Baldwin was 66, Ramsay Macdonald and the Belgian Socialist leader Emile Vandervelde 67, Hindenburg 86. Hitler and Mussolini were 44, Mosley 37, Doriot 35, Codreanu 31, José Antonio 30, Degrelle 24. Figures like these speak for themselves. (*See Reading No. 5A.*)

In a profounder sense, however, a revolutionary movement must recruit people who are all free in social position or in spirit. One cannot take great risks, run the chance of scandal or arrest, be available for anything at all hours, if the thought of career or mortgage or an income holds one back. Only the very poor, the very young (also perhaps the very rich, but there are few of those and even fewer who want to change the order from which they benefit), can qualify for revolutionary action, as opposed to writing or to talk; and they envisage it quite often as a way of ceasing to be nonentities or to be poor. The danger that the activist flame may be stifled by public position or material concerns is one all revolutionary parties face; and they resolve it by elitism, and by decreeing that the gains of any victory shall be not particular but collective. They follow up their idealistic appeal with the attempt to connect private success with that of the collective and to keep the militant from acquiring such vested interests in the *status quo* as to lose interest in continued revolution. Then, as and when they can, they do their best to train the youth to transfer its self-interest from self to Party, that is to the nation.

Meanwhile, like all minority movements, the Fascists can only succeed when social circumstances provide a public their appeal attracts or, at least, the resources that will help them win it. This was what happened to the *fascios,* to the Nazis and, briefly, to the French leagues of the middle twenties. In France, however, as in Britain and Belgium, conditions never became bad enough for a tide of sympathy to float the local movements into power. Fascist and National Socialist movements were fated to remain minoritarian and (while their doctrine often incorporated measures we should call progressive) to win only by violence or to disappear. Alternately, a Fascist movement whose revolutionary and "social" character made it popular enough to attain power by legal means might be suppressed, as in Romania, by conservative forces, suspected and kept at arm's length as in Hungary, or used and then crushed as in Spain. In any case, the identification between Fascism and reaction is widely off the mark.

The identification of Fascism and National Socialism is more understandable and better justified. It should be possible, however, to distinguish between the two, even if only at the doctrinal level. For, while what people say about their ideas does not always match what they actually do, it does reflect their assumptions, and it is usually respected—if only in the breach.

Fascism. Fascism, as must be clear by now, rejects theory in favor of practice and relies largely on the attraction of that "fever" to which I have referred. The Fascist ethos is emotional and sentimental: at that level the ends of action count less than action itself, and the forces that lead men into the Fascist camp can be enlisted on any side whatever, provided they are given an opportunity to indulge themselves—the more violent, the better. This indiscriminate nature of Fascism appears in figures as far apart as Mussolini, Doriot, and Degrelle, who militated in turn in a number of parties, pursuing action rather than ideas, power rather than principles.

National Socialism. The National Socialist, on the other hand, seems much more theoretical. He may use theory merely to rationalize, but he respects it. Whatever he may pretend, words and ideas count for him as much as actions, and sometimes they replace them. What men like Déat seem to have sought was a new *system* which, unlike old ones that had been tried and found wanting, would help rebuild or repair the failing structure of the state.

Although the program of the Arrow Cross or of the Iron Guard was profoundly mystical, the spirit animating such movements was of a different order from that which we find in the *fascios* or in Rex. A doctrine may be crackpot though dogmatic: the theories of Rosenberg, of Szalasi, of Quisling, were both; but they differ less among themselves than they do from the cheerful pragmatism of Mussolini or Degrelle.

All this may mean that the ideological National Socialist (the kind we may, for instance, find in France) will content himself with theorizing, but never go beyond the grandiose plans and dire threats he lavishes in print. It also lays him open to the charge (as brought against the Nazis) of using his theories as bait for the unwary, while in practice he advances through deals with the forces of capital, which are perhaps using him after all, as John Strachey suggested. It is quite obvious, however, that the Nazis of all people were ready to make the most extraordinary sacrifices for the sake of their theories and their twisted ideals.

It is true that Hitler was an opportunist who declared his aims very clearly and very early in the game, and then temporized on their accomplishment. But the deals and the sacrifices that he made, first to get into power and then to affirm his power, were expedients he abandoned as soon as possible. Industrialists like Fritz Thyssen, conservatives like Franz von Papen, moderate economists like Schacht, moderate diplomats like Neurath were shed, or brought to heel, or crushed, as and when circumstances permitted; likewise the army. True, about 1927 and again in 1934, Hitler toned down the radical aspect of his movement in order to win the support of conservative forces that he had to conciliate. But in the next decade the Nazi state affirmed its control ever more totally over every sector of national life and, had it won the war, there would have been little that escaped its direction, little that remained private except in name.

Differences. This, then, is where the basic difference seems to lie: Fascism is pragmatically activist, National Socialism theoretically motivated or, at least, expressed. Both aim to conquer power and that center of power which is the modern state. But in one case the power will be wielded pragmatically and piecemeal, simply for its own sake, while the party which has been its instrument may gradually be abandoned. In the other, power will be used to realize an anterior plan or a series of plans inspired by the original doctrine; and then the party may become a Church—a Church and a dynamo.

Therein lie the nature and the major characteristics of movements which between them encompass a vast area of contemporary experience. Conceived in Europe, like Nationalism and Marxism, Fascism and National Socialism have become articles for export. The circumstances in which they grew, the sentiments that inspired them, the characteristics we have noted, may be found with variations in most political situations of the world today. Neither sympathy nor dislike are by themselves a satisfactory reaction to attitudes and ideas with which we must learn to cope. Fascist movements demand further investigation if we are to understand the many problems which confront us here and now.

Part II

READINGS

— Reading No. 1 —

FASCISM

The selections in this reading are taken both from friendly and from hostile sources, and they suggest the variety of guises in which Fascism may appear.

The first program of the Fascist movement, which reflects its early revolutionary tone, contrasts with the highly empirical approach of Mussolini in his famous discussion of Fascist doctrine. The Communist analysis of Fascist phenomena, on the other hand, seems at least partially borne out by the views of Wyndham Lewis, a British painter and writer (1884-1957), who was attracted by the more reactionary aspects of Fascism, although he expresses his sympathy in radical terms.

This contradictory aspect is one of the chief characteristics of Fascism, and one which a comparison between the many statements that follow and the movements they represent will bear out.

1   *1*   *1*

A. FIRST PROGRAM OF THE FASCIST MOVEMENT: MARCH 23, 1919 *

1. A national Constituent Assembly, Italian section of the international Constituent Assembly of nations, which will proceed to a radical transformation of the political and economic foundations of collective life.

2. Proclamation of the Italian Republic. Decentralization of executive power; autonomous administration of regions and municipalities by their own legislative bodies. Sovereignty of the people exercised by means of universal, equal and direct

* Quoted in *Le Fascisme en Italie* (Paris: 1934), pp. 14-15.

145

suffrage, by all citizens of both sexes, the people keeping the right of initiative for referendum and veto.

3. Abolition of the Senate. Suppression of political police. Election of magistrates independently of the executive power.

4. Suppression of all titles of nobility and orders of knighthood.

5. Suppression of compulsory military service.

6. Freedom of opinion, of conscience and of belief, freedom of association and of the press.

7. An educational system, general and professional, open to all.

8. A maximum of public health measures.

9. Suppression of limited liability companies and shareholding companies; suppression of all forms of speculation; supression of Banks and Stock Exchanges.

10. Census and taxation of private wealth. Confiscation of unproductive revenues.

11. Prohibition of child labor under the age of 16. Eight-hour day.

12. Reorganization of production according to the cooperative principle, including the workers' direct share of profits.

13. Abolition of secret diplomacy.

14. Foreign policy inspired by international solidarity and national independence within a Confederation of States.

B. PROGRAM OF THE COMMUNIST INTERNATIONAL, 1928: DEFINITION OF FASCISM *

Under certain special historical conditions the progress of the bourgeois, imperialist, reactionary offensive assumes the form of Fascism.

These conditions are: instability of capital relationships; the existence of considerable declassed social elements, the pauperization of broad strata of the urban petit-bourgeoisie and of the intelligentsia; discontent among the rural petit-bourgeoisie, and, finally, the constant menace of mass proletarian action. In order to stabilize and perpetuate its rule the bourgeoisie is compelled to an increasing degree to abandon the parliamentary system in favor of the Fascist system, which is independent of inter-party arrangements and combinations.

The Fascist system is a system of direct dictatorship, ideologically masked by the "national idea" and representation of the "professions" (in reality, representation of the various groups of the ruling class). It is a system that resorts to a peculiar form of social demagogy (anti-Semitism, occasional

* Quoted in R. Palme Dutt, *Fascism and Social Revolution,* Lawrence and Wishart Ltd. (London: 1934), pp. 88-89.

sorties against usurer's capital and gestures of impatience with the parliamentary "talking shop") in order to use the discontent of the petit-bourgeoisie, the intelligentsia, and other strata of society; and to corruption through the building up of a compact and well-paid hierarchy of Fascist units, a party apparatus and a bureaucracy. At the same time, Fascism strives to permeate the working class by recruiting the most backward strata of the workers to its ranks, by playing upon their discontent, by taking advantage of the inaction of Social Democracy, etc.

The principal aim of Fascism is to destroy the revolutionary labor vanguard, i.e., the Communist sections and leading units of the proletariat. The combination of social demagogy, corruption and active White terror, in conjunction with extreme imperialist aggression in the sphere of foreign politics, are the characteristic features of Fascism. In periods of acute crisis for the bourgeois, Fascism resorts to anti-capitalist phraseology, but, after it has established itself at the helm of the State, it casts aside its anti-capitalist rattle and discloses itself as a terrorist dictatorship of big capital.

C. Benito Mussolini: THE POLITICAL AND SOCIAL DOCTRINE OF FASCISM, 1932 *

When, in the now distant March of 1919, I summoned a meeting at Milan . . . of the surviving members of the Interventionist Party who had themselves been in action, and who had followed me since the creation of the Fascist Revolutionary Party (of 1915), I had no specific doctrinal attitude in mind. I had a living experience of one doctrine only—that of Socialism, from 1903-4 to the winter of 1914—that is to say, about a decade: and from Socialism itself, even though I have taken part in the movement first as a member of the rank and file and later as a leader, yet I had no experience of its doctrine of action. A unanimous, universally accepted theory of Socialism did not exist after 1905. . . . In the great stream of Fascism are to be found ideas which began with Sorel, Péguy, with Lagardelle in the "Mouvement Socialiste," and with the Italian trade union movement which throughout the period of 1904-14 was sounding a new note in Italian Socialist circles. . . .

After the war, in 1919, Socialism was already dead as a doctrine: it existed only as hatred. The *Popolo d'Italia* was then given the subtitle of "The newspaper of ex-servicemen and

* From Benito Mussolini, "The Political and Social Doctrine of Fascism," in *International Conciliation,* No. 306 (January 1935), pp. 5-17. Reprinted by permission of the Carnegie Endowment for International Peace.

producers," and the word "producers" was already the expression of a mental attitude. Fascism was not the nursling of a doctrine worked out beforehand with detailed elaboration; it was born of the need for action and it was itself from the beginning practical rather than theoretical; it was not merely another political party but, even in the first two years, in opposition to all political parties as such. . . . If one were to re-read . . . the report of the meeting in which the *Fasci Italiani di combattimento* were constituted, one would there find no ordered expression of doctrine, but a series of aphorisms, anticipations, and aspirations which, when refined by time from the original ore, were destined after some years to develop into an ordered series of doctrinal concepts, forming the Fascists' political doctrine—different from all others either of the past or the present day.

"If the bourgeoisie," I said then, "think that they will find lightning-rods in us, they are the more deceived; we must start work at once. . . . We want to accustom the working-class to real and effectual leadership, and also to convince them that it is no easy thing to direct an industry or a commercial enterprise successfully. . . . We shall combat every retrograde idea, technical or spiritual. . . . When the succession to the seat of government is open, we must not be unwilling to fight for it. We must make haste; when the present regime breaks down, we must be ready at once to take its place. It is we who have the right to the succession, because it was we who forced the country into the War, and led her to victory. The present method of political representation cannot suffice, we must have a representation direct from the individuals concerned. It may be objected against this program that it is a return to the conception of the corporation, but that is no matter. . . . Therefore, I desire that this assembly shall accept the claims of national trades-unionism from the economic point of view. . . ."

Now is it not a singular thing that even on this first day in the Piazza San Sepolcro that word "corporation" arose, which later, in the course of the Revolution, came to express one of the creations of social legislation at the very foundation of the regime?

The years which preceded the March to Rome were years of great difficulty, during which the necessity for action did not permit of research or any complete elaboration of doctrine. The battle had to be fought in the towns and villages. There was much discussion, but—what was more important and more sacred—men died. They knew how to die. Doctrine, beautifully defined and carefully elucidated, with headlines and paragraphs, might be lacking; but there was to take its place something more decisive—Faith. . . . But, since there was inevitably some lack of system, the adversaries of Fascism have disingenuously denied that it had any capacity to produce a doctrine of its own, though that doctrine was growing and taking shape under their very eyes, even though tumultuously; first, as happens to all ideas in their beginnings, in the aspect of a violent and dogmatic negation, and then in the aspect of positive construction which has found its realization in the laws and institutions of the regime as enacted successively in the years 1926, 1927 and 1928. . . .

Above all, Fascism, the more it considers and observes the future and the development of humanity quite apart from political considerations of the moment, believes neither in the possibility nor the utility of perpetual peace. It thus repudiates the doctrine of Pacifism—born of a renunciation of the struggle and an act of cowardice in the face of sacrifice. War alone brings up to its highest tension all human energy and puts the stamp of nobility upon the peoples who have the courage to meet it. All other trials are substitutes, which never really put men into the position where they have to make the great decision—the alternative of life or death. Thus a doctrine which is founded upon this harmful postulate of peace is hostile to Fascism. And thus hostile to the spirit of Fascism . . . are all the international leagues and societies which, as history will show, can be scattered to the winds when once strong national feeling is aroused by any motive—sentimental, ideal, or practical. This anti-pacifist spirit is carried by Fascism even into the life of the individual; the proud motto of the Squadrista, *"Me ne frego"* (I do not fear), written on the bandage of the wound, is an act of philosophy not only stoic, the summary of a doctrine not only political—it is the education to combat, the acceptance of the risks which combat implies, and a new way of life for Italy. Thus the Fascist accepts life and loves it, knowing nothing of and despising suicide; he rather conceives of life as duty and struggle and conquest, life which should be high and full, lived for oneself, but above all for others—those who are at hand and those who are far distant, contemporaries, and those who will come after. . . .

Such a conception of life makes Fascism the complete opposite of that doctrine, the base of the so-called scientific and Marxian Socialism, the materialist conception of history; according to which the history of human civilization can be explained simply through the conflict of interests among the various social groups and by the change and development in the means and instruments of production. That the changes in the economic field . . . have their importance no one can deny; but that these factors are sufficient to explain the history of humanity excluding all others is an absurd delusion. Fascism,

now and always, believes in holiness and in heroism; that is to
say, in actions influenced by no economic motive, direct or
indirect. And if the economic conception of history be denied
. . . it follows that the existence of an unchangeable and un-
changing class war is also denied. And above all Fascism denies
that class war can be the preponderant force in the transformation of society. These two fundamental concepts of Socialism
being thus refuted, nothing is left of it but the sentimental aspiration—as old as humanity itself—towards a social convention in which the sorrows and sufferings of the humblest shall
be alleviated. But here again Fascism repudiates the conception
of "economic" happiness . . . Fascism denies the materialist
conception of happiness as a possibility, and abandons it to
its inventors, the economists of the first half of the nineteenth
century: that is to say, Fascism denies the validity of the equation, wellbeing = happiness, which would reduce men to the
level of animals, caring for one thing only—to be fat and well-
fed—and would thus degrade humanity to a purely physical
existence.

After Socialism, Fascism combats the whole complex system
of democratic ideology; and repudiates it, whether in its theoretical premises or in its practical application. Fascism denies
that the majority, by the simple fact that it is a majority, can
direct human society; it denies that numbers alone can govern
by means of a periodical consultation, and it affirms the im-
mutable, beneficial, and fruitful inequality of mankind, which
can never be permanently leveled through the mere operation
of a mechanical process such as universal suffrage. The democratic regime may be defined as from time to time giving the
people the illusion of sovereignty, while the real effective
sovereignty lies in the hands of other concealed and irresponsible forces. Democracy is a regime nominally without a king,
but it is ruled by many kings—more absolute, tyrannical, and
ruinous than one sole king, even though a tyrant. This explains
why Fascism, having first in 1922 (for reasons of expediency)
assumed an attitude tending towards republicanism, renounced
this point of view before the March to Rome; being convinced that the question of political form is not today of prime
importance. . . .

A party which entirely governs a nation is a fact entirely
new to history, there are no possible references or parallels.
Fascism uses in its construction whatever elements in the
Liberal, Social, or Democratic doctrines still have a living
value; it maintains what may be called the certainties which we
owe to history, but it rejects all the rest—that is to say, the conception that there can be any doctrine of unquestioned efficacy
for all times and all peoples. . . . Political doctrines pass, but

humanity remains; and it may rather be expected that this will be a century of Fascism. For if the nineteenth century was the century of individualism (Liberalism always signifying individualism) it may be expected that this will be the century of collectivism, and hence the century of the State. . . .

Every doctrine tends to direct human activity towards a determined objective; but the action of men also reacts upon the doctrine, transforms it, adapts it to new needs, or supersedes it with something else. A doctrine then must be no mere exercise in words, but a living act; and thus the value of Fascism lies in the fact that it is veined with pragmatism, but at the same time has a will to exist and a will to power, a firm front in face of the reality of "violence."

The foundation of Fascism is the conception of the State. Fascism conceives of the State as an absolute, in comparison with which all individuals or groups are relative, only to be conceived of in their relation to the State. . . .

The Fascist State has drawn into itself even the economic activities of the nation, and through the corporative social and educational institutions created by it, its influence reaches every aspect of the national life and includes, framed in their respective organizations, all the political, economic and spiritual forces of the nation. A State which reposes upon the support of millions of individuals who recognize its authority, are continually conscious of its power and are ready at once to serve it, is not the old tyrannical State of the medieval lord nor has it anything in common with the absolute governments either before or after 1789. The individual in the Fascist State is not annulled but rather multiplied, just in the same way that a soldier in a regiment is not diminished but rather increased by the number of his comrades. The Fascist State organizes the nation, but leaves a sufficient margin of liberty to the individual; the latter is deprived of all useless and possibly harmful freedom, but retains what is essential. . . .

The Fascist State is an embodied will to power and government; the Roman tradition is here an ideal of force in action. According to Fascism, government is not so much a thing to be expressed in territorial or military terms as in terms of morality and the spirit. It must be thought of as an empire— that is to say, a nation which directly or indirectly rules other nations, without the need for conquering a single square yard of territory. For Fascism, the growth of empire, that is to say the expansion of the nation, is an essential manifestation of vitality, and its opposite a sign of decadence. Peoples which are rising, or rising again after a period of decadence, are always imperialist: any renunciation is a sign of decay and of death.

Fascism is the doctrine best adapted to represent the tendencies and the aspirations of a people, like the people of Italy, who are rising again after many centuries of abasement and foreign servitude. But empire demands discipline, the co-ordination of all forces and a deeply felt sense of duty and sacrifice; this fact explains many aspects of the practical working of the regime, the character of many forces in the State, and the necessarily severe measures which must be taken against those who would oppose this spontaneous and inevitable movement of Italy in the 20th century, and would oppose it by recalling the outworn ideology of the nineteenth century . . . for never before has the nation stood more in need of authority, of direction, and of order. If every age has its own characteristic doctrine, there are a thousand signs which point to Fascism as the characteristic doctrine of our time. For if a doctrine must be a living thing, this is proved by the fact that Fascism has created a living faith; and that this faith is very powerful in the minds of men, is demonstrated by those who have suffered and died for it.

D. Wyndham Lewis: FASCISM *

You stand today where Socialism stood yesterday—for the Poor against the Rich. You do not stand against Property: you are reproached for that, but you should in fact be congratulated upon it. For today it is above all the Rich (the super-rich) who are against property, since money has merged into power, the concrete into the abstract. For the men of the French Revolution property was a prerequisite of freedom, and they were better revolutionaries than their successors today. To keep property was one of the cardinal points of their program. No "proletarian," no workman, would ever know freedom again, if there were nothing in the world but himself and his kind, and over him and his kind the great bureaucratic oligarchs, or commissars, and their swarms of delators and armed servants.

You as a Fascist stand for the small trader against the chainstore; for the peasant against the usurer; for the nation, great or small, against the super-state; for personal business against Big Business; for the craftsman against the machine; for the creator against the middleman; for all that prospers by individual effort and creative toil, against all that prospers in the abstract air of High Finance or of the theoretical ballyhoo of Internationalism.

* Wyndham Lewis, "Left Wings and the C3 Mind." *British Union Quarterly,* Vol. I, No. 1, January-April 1937, pp. 32-33.

RACIALIST NATIONAL SOCIALISM

All National Socialism is nationalistic, as the name implies, but not all of it is racially exclusive. The best-known variety of such racialist fanaticism arose in Germany and Scandinavia where, between the wars, popular and racial self-expression were merged into one very dynamic movement which pretended to guarantee social and economic justice for the in-group, at the expense of all outsiders, particularly Jews, who appeared as the incarnation of the disruptive alien elements these creeds shun.

The passages which follow show the transition from the early and matter-of-fact statement of such views to an increasingly metaphysical and crackpot vision of sombre and diabolic forces at work in history.

The first program of the Nazi Party is taken from the excellent presentation of National-Socialism *prepared by Raymond E. Murphy and published by the United States Department of State in 1943. The brief quotation from Nazism's leading doctrinaire, Alfred Rosenberg, is designed to mark the transition to the strange rhetoric of the Norwegian apostle of racialism, Vidkun Quisling, whose anti-Communism gave him the ear of many respectable men in the West before his wartime collaboration with the German invaders of his land provided a new term for treachery.*

✓ ✓ ✓

A. THE FIRST PROGRAM OF THE NAZI PARTY *

None but members of the nation may be citizens of the State. None but those of German blood, whatever their creed, may be members of the nation. No Jew, therefore, may be a member of the nation.

Anyone who is not a citizen of the State may live in Germany only as a guest and must be regarded as being subject to foreign laws.

We demand that the State shall make it its first duty to promote the industry and livelihood of its citizens. If it is not possible to nourish the entire population of the State, foreign nationals must be excluded. . . .

* *From The Twenty-Five Points of the NSDAP, 1920,* quoted in Raymond E. Murphy, *National-Socialism,* U.S. Department of State (1943).

It must be the first duty of every citizen to work with his mind or with his body. The activities of the individual may not clash with the interests of the whole, but must proceed within the frame of the community and be for the general good. We demand therefore: abolition of incomes unearned by work . . . ruthless confiscation of all war profits . . . nationalisation of all trusts . . . sharing out of profits from wholesale trade . . . extensive development of provisions for old age . . . immediate communalization of wholesale business premises and their lease at low rates to small traders . . . land reform . . . uncompensated confiscation of land for communal purposes, abolition of interest on land loans and prevention of all speculation in land . . . ruthless prosecution of all whose activities are injurious to the common interest. . . .

We demand legal warfare against conscious political lying and its dissemination in the Press . . . a German national Press . . . all German-language newspaper editors and their assistants must be members of the nation . . . special permission shall be necessary for non-German newspapers [*in German or not*] . . . non-Germans shall be prohibited by law from financial participation in or influence over German newspapers. . . .

The publication of papers not conducive to the national welfare must be forbidden. We demand legal prosecution of all literary and artistic tendencies likely to disintegrate our national life, and the suppression of institutions which militate against its needs.

We demand liberty for all religious denominations . . . which present no danger to the State or militate against the moral feelings of the German race. The Party, as such, stands for positive Christianity, but does not bind itself . . . to any particular confession. It fights the Jewish-materialist spirit within us and outside, and is convinced that our nation can only achieve permanent health . . . on the principle: THE COMMON INTEREST BEFORE SELF.

That all the foregoing may be realized, we demand the creation of a strong central State power, undisputed authority of the politically-centralized Parliament over the entire Reich . . . and formation of Chambers for classes and professions, which will carry out the laws promulgated by the Reich. . . .

The leaders of the Party swear to go forward unswervingly, if necessary at the cost of their lives, to secure the fulfilment of these points.

B. Alfred Rosenberg:
THE MYTH OF THE TWENTIETH CENTURY (1930)*

History and vocation no longer consist in struggle of class against class, church dogma against dogma, but in the struggle between blood and blood, race and race, people and people. And this means: values of soul fight against values of soul. That history must be judged from the point of view of race is a truth which will soon be self-evident. . . . But the values of the *soul* of race, which are the motive powers behind the new philosophy, are not yet part of actual general knowledge. Now soul means race seen from within. Conversely, race is the outside of a soul. To call to life the soul of race is to recognize its supreme value and, under its guidance, to give the other values their organic position: in state, religion, and in art. This is the task of our century: to create a new type of man out of a new myth of life. . . .

In the midst of the most terrible collapse, the old Nordic soul of race wakes up to new, higher consciousness. It sees at last that different—and necessarily mutually exclusive—supreme values must not co-exist with equal rights. . . . It sees that what is related to its soul and race may be fitted in, but that the foreign must be ruthlessly rejected and, if need be, fought down. Not because it is "wrong" or "bad" in itself, but because it is foreign to the kind and destroys the internal construction of our nature.

C. Vidkun Quisling: THE NORDIC PRINCIPLE †

The Nordic Principle rests on Nordic traditions, Nordic thought and constructive co-operation, in contrast to Jewish liberalism and Marxism, which promote their destructive purposes by means of hatred, envy and class war for their own ends.

One is allied to the Divine; the other to the diabolical.

The spiritual power of the Nordic principle is, therefore, stronger and deeper than the Marxist-materialist view of existence which is threatening our race and civilization with destruction.

It is in reality our intrinsic national Principle to which we must adhere and which we must realize with inexorable consistency.

* From Michael Oakeshott, *The Social and Political Doctrines of Contemporary Europe,* Cambridge University Press (Cambridge: 1939), pp. 200-201.
† From Vidkun Quisling, "A Nordic World Federation," *British Union Quarterly,* Vol. I, No. 1, January-April 1937, pp. 100-101.

It is also my conviction that, when we recognize the profound truths of the historic past as well as the historic present, and see the great things accomplished by people of Nordic race from the beginning of history until our day, when they are more powerful than ever before; and when, at the same time, we are convinced that the Divine Will is revealed in the historical course of world development, we must, without under-estimating the importance and contribution of others, be permitted to believe in the continued historical and divine mission of the Nordic peoples in the world. As in times past, it must be the mission of our great family of peoples to do away with an obsolete world and create a new world which can place the whole human family on the upward grade.

The *Nasjonal Samling* invites all people of Nordic race and outlook in every country—Norwegians, Swedes, Danes, Icelanders, Britons, Germans and Dutch and all others of Nordic blood and spirit—to unite in a Nordic World Movement to create peace and cooperation between all Nordic peoples throughout the world and to carry on the struggle for the salvation and progress of our civilization.

— Reading No. 3 —

HUNGARY

The following pages are culled from the writings of Hungary's leading National Socialist, Ferencz Szalasi, considered in his time as one of the best officers of the Hungarian General Staff. My translator assures me that any incoherence to be found below is only a pale reflection of the original, which steadfastly ignores grammar, style and sense.

Since Szalasi graduated with honors from the Hungarian War College, it is clear that military and literary capacity do not always go together. Yet hundreds of thousands of Hungarians, not all of them illiterate, put their faith in Szalasi, and one must assume that they failed to read his magnum opus (*only about 60 pages long*), *just as the Germans neglected to read* Mein Kampf.

To complete his statement of 1936, I have added a brief

excerpt from the remarks he made in court upon being condemned to death for treachery in 1946. The oracular quality of such utterances seems to reflect both his extraordinary confidence and the progressive derangement of his mind.

✓   ✓   ✓

A. Ferencz Szalasi:
THE WAY AND THE AIM *

Hungarism is an ideological system. It is the Hungarian practice of the national socialistic view of the world and time spirit.

Not Hitlerism, not fascism, not antisemitism, but Hungarism.

Thus Hungarism means socialism, the tuning together of the moral, spiritual, and material interests of the I and the Us. It has set as its aim not the happiness of the particular privileged individuals or classes, but of the totality of individuals and classes. But Hungarism at the same time also means national socialism, because it fights for the happiness of the most natural community of the people, for the welfare of the nation and through this of every working individual. Hungarism is not designed for the "Mutilated country," neither is it merely designed for the needs of the Hungarian people, but for all the nationalities who live in the Danube basin surrounded by the Carpathian mountains, who are worthy of a country and earth to grow roots in, and who, under the direction and guidance of the Hungarian people, and with them, compose the social, economic, moral, spiritual, material and political unity of the Hungarian nation.

Besides all this, Hungarism is the protector of all the members of its national family who are strewn all over the world and have been forced out [*of their country*] by the need to earn a livelihood. Its right and duty is their repatriation into the Great Fatherland.

Hungarism assures peace for the Hungarians and groups of nations living here, the Pax Hungarica, in the Carpathian Danube basin not only by giving a Fatherland and a home to the groups of peoples, furthermore by giving cultural autonomy (language, popular education, self-government and justice, within the framework of self-government and the self-determination of economic interest groups) all these are assured for them within its system of allegiance, but also it will sanction through popular elections based on free assertion of their will, the moral, spiritual, and material well being of the national groups living within the Carpathian Danube basin under the jurisdiction of the Hungarian people. . . .

* From Ferencz Szalasi, *Ut es Cél* (Budapest: 1936), translated by Anne M. Sail.

The basis for this inner peace will be the workpeace of all working classes who live within the nation. This workpeace will hold in inseparable national unity the peasant who supports the nation, the worker who builds the nation, the intelligentsia which leads the nation, the soldier who defends the nation, and the tokens of national immortality: women and youth. Furthermore, it creates: 1. The economic peace which proportionately divides the profits of labor and production between the factors of production, in order to abolish money capitalism and the hopeless misery of the working class. 2. Social peace which ignores privileged classes: feudal, clerical, and liberal capitalist ruling class, upper, middle and lower class, but rather the united socialist community of the workers; and 3. Political peace which does not mislead the political nation with selfish party interests, but in which a single leading political idea directs the community to ensure the welfare of the nation within the community of other European nations. . . .

During history three totalities have developed, first successively and later parallel to each other and strengthening each other. Their common feature is that they demand unconditional obedience, each representing a most ancient dictatorship within a closed society. The oldest is the military totality. Later came the totality of the Church. And after that the economic totality of the leaders of economic life—mainly Jews. Thus morality, spirit, and material things have separately found their most typical representatives, they have progressed separately, but in their great decisions we always find them together.

In national socialism, however, the fourth totality was born: the totality of the nation. This is the most perfect totality, because it can unite the others. The envious dwarfs have looked will ill favor upon the new-born Hercules, they have perceived the threatening fact that this great newborn can by himself unite and fulfill their moral, spiritual and material beings which had, up to now, developed separately: the religious totality as a fact of national morality, the military totality as the armed nation, the totality of the private economy as national socialist communal well-being. It follows that the fight between them and ourselves is inevitable. And it is indeed a fact that Italy and Germany, which pioneered in national socialism, have been opposed by the three other totalities, the enemies of the national totality.

In the final development of the victorious national socialist struggle, it is interesting to see how the separate fights resulted: the Church withdraws its political divisions from the fight and, keeping them in reserve for better times, it comes to terms; the armed forces are absorbed into the armed nation and come to their broadest fulfillment; and the totality of private economy is annihilated. . . . Thus, when we foresee the results of our own victory, we must remember that of the three totalities we can only expect understanding from the military totality, this being the one which really gains and attains its most perfect development with the victory of national socialism. . . .

The past world war demanded immeasurable sacrifices from the opposing parties in human lives on the battlefronts and in material goods behind the front lines. The peace treaties which followed did not bring quiescence, merely armistice in which hundreds of thousands bled to death, and millions lost their daily bread.

Big capital having only gained in the war, wanted to continue its activities where it left off in 1914. The lords of big capital dared to believe that the enrichment which for some was the result of the war, bought by the blood and sufferings of millions, could not only be maintained but greatly increased.

Some military leaders understood the war. The peace had no experts. And while France demanded gold payments from Germany of such magnitude that they exceeded the amount of gold in existence, the United States, forgetting the alliance, forced France into stiff payments. France could not fulfill her obligation, but could not transfer it either, and thus the whole world, creditor and debtor alike, was in an unsettled "pending" position.

National socialism is the expert of peace, of everybody's peace. Its executor: the Nation. One of the most important tasks of national socialism is the just balancing of the inequality of fortunes, the abolition of the artificial obstacles that paralyze our economic life, and the prevention of the immoral amassing of fortunes based on abuses and called "extremely clever."

We must not fear that the Hungarian national socialist economy will harm the talent, the diligence, and the know-how of the nation, because it will only limit that extremely unjust process of getting rich which in its present form leads to an orgy of the degeneration of millions. The Hungarian national socialist economy is inseparable from the Hungarian national socialist moral and spiritual life; its aim being the material welfare of the community of the people. *Thus our national economy and its every part is a means and not an end. . . .*

We cannot bring our fight against the obsolete system of private capital to victory without solving the Jewish question. The realization of the Hungarian national socialist economic system and the solution of the Jewish question are inseparable, one follows from the other, the two tasks are two sides of the same coin.

As a result of our successful work of enlightenment liberal private capitalism has little by little only Jewish followers left.

In spite of this the objection is still, though ever more rarely, heard in intellectual circles—especially on the part of the leading intellectuals who have been forced upon the nation, that the solution of the Jewish question by "the German system" would result for this country in upsetting the economic and financial order from one day to the next and that the country's economy and finance could not survive this for a single day. Such a statement is either a fool-hardy lie or criminal stupidity which leads to the misleading, to the ruin, and to the death of the nation. Let there be an end, once and for all to the official superstition that Hungarian life without Jews is unimaginable. Truly, the Hungarian national community can exist without the Jew. Anyhow we shall solve the Jewish question not according to a "foreign system," since the totality of our national socialist practice does not develop according to a foreign system, but according to our peculiar national circumstances and Hungarian national abilities.

It is true that the forcing of the solution of the Jewish question in the years 1919-1920 would have bankrupted the country, because of our isolation. Today however, our national economy can be transferred into Hungarian hands without a hitch, since almost every one of our neighbours is ruled by the national socialist system. . . . It is also quite clear to us that in the purification of our economic life not only the solution of the Jewish question is essential, but also the exclusion of those Christian Hungarians contaminated by the economic spirit of the Jewry. These will have to be relieved and retired. We shall dare to do this because in our economic knowledge and economic abilities we shall not be guided by the spirit of Jewish morality, but by the life-force, resourcefulness and will for life of our Hungarian people. We shall continue with our indoctrination to ripen the majestic theories of Hungarian national socialism for this transformation. Against those whom enlightenment cannot change, or those who use the slogans of socialism to play their obscene game of filling their pockets, we shall employ the whip. . . .

In the crystallization of Hungarism the "socialnational" is that ideological system which

—assures for every worker of the Nation within the Hungarian national socialist brotherhood and community of faith employment and a living and thus creates for the workers of the Nation a secure and worker loving nation:

—provides an ideological basis for the workers of all national socialist states and communities of people for the appropriate fulfillment of their socialism and for its practical establishment:

—safeguards, assures, and legalizes the obligation to work

in the work-order, and the right to work in the national economy:

—fulfills socialism within the body of the nation in its moral, spiritual, and material totality:

—fights for a nationally conscious national community for the workers of the Danube basin surrounded by the Carpathians, a community which is built on work, on right and on appreciation. . . .

The socialism of liberalism is capital socialism, the socialism of Marxism is state socialism, while the socialism of the socialnational is national socialism. In liberalism the state serves the individual, the individual serves capital; in Marxism the individual serves the state and the state serves capital; while in the socialnational capital serves the state, the state serves the nation, and the moral, spiritual, and material interests and values of the national community serve without exceptions for the good and benefit of its every member. . . .

The basic tenet of our national economic system:

Capital amassed by one man has a limit. Above this limit capital is not the fruit of one man's labor. The working nation has contributed to its amassing with production, the millions of the national community with consumption, and the state power by ensuring production, consumption and the enjoyment of profits by the will of the nation. Thus the Hungarian national socialist state power has a right to exert an influence in the utilization, production, the enjoyment of the profit of capital communally amassed and to provide a just share from the blessed profits of the capital for the participants in such a way that this division of the shares should serve the community of the people through its material interests, its moral and spiritual interests as well. . . .

The Worker

The Worker is a nationbuilder.

The road to the peasant leads through nature. To the worker through ideology.

Many forks of the road lead towards the peasant, everyone of which can be travelled without the need to bury and annihilate the others. But to the worker, there are only two roads: the road of the old ideology, and the road of the new ideology. When one has reached its end the other will be destroyed by itself. This is the difference when the national socialist movement starts to tackle the two largest strata of our national community.

The road which leads to the peasant is by its nature more tactical, the road which leads to the worker is more strategic: thus the first can be conquered with practical weapons, and

the second with spiritual weapons. This is the first basic law of
our labor movement. We must make the peasant practice
Hungarian national socialism, and we must make the worker
conscious of it, because after it has become evident he will
practice it himself. This is the second basic law of our labor
movement. From our point of view, the peasant is not an active
factor, because he only accepts and fights for that which has
already proven itself. . . . The worker . . . will fight to bring
victory to the ideology of which he has become innerly conscious, in order to make it into a really practical system. It
follows from this that every ideology has become victorious
as soon as it has been accepted by the workers. . . . This is
the third basic law of our labor movement.

The peasantry can be drawn into a new system in partial
groups and slowly moulded into the new framework. The
worker breaks away voluntarily and consciously from the old
ideology, annihilates it entirely, and throws himself with great
élan into the new patterns that the ideology provides. He does
not lose his strength even temporarily, on the contrary he
increases it, because he knows, professes and believes that the
new ideology as opposed to the old means greater strength
for him. This is the fourth law of our labor movement. The
inner and practical life of the peasant is outspokenly egocentric
socialism, whose most fertile aspect is the socialization of the
land. He cannot develop his socialism further. The inner and
practical life of the worker is all-encompassing, and it includes
the whole community of the nation. Thus the socialism of the
worker is a folk and social socialism. This is the fifth law of
our labor movement. . . .

The working class is dissatisfied, and this is essential because
of the bankruptcy of its Marxist ideologies. It had to be disillusioned with the system it believed in, from which it hoped,
for which it fought, and from which it expected its welfare. It
does not know what to do with the bankrupt mass of its Marxist
ideology, which stifles and pushes it into moral, spiritual and
material annihilation. It would not accept the Marxist ideology
any more, even if Communism were to reappear in our Fatherland. This is the sixth law of our labor movement, and at the
same time the most important, because the knowledge of this
provides our movement with an excellent fighting weapon.

The purpose of our Hungarist movement is to win over the
Hungarian working class to the Hungarian national socialist
ideology. . . .

The Intelligentsia

The intelligentsia is the leader of the Nation and guides it.
The road to the peasant leads through nature, to the worker

through the destruction of his old ideology. To the intelligentsia through the restoration of its faith, of its self-esteem, and of the elevating awareness of a calling, through its inner and bodily rebirth.

We emphasize that by intelligentsia we do not mean only the middle classes. They are only an element of the intelligentsia, within the collective idea of which belong all those who through conscious intellect have deserved the responsible direction and leadership of some community with their personal knowledge and action.

Thus the peasantry and the working class have their intelligentsia, just as some layers of the middle class lack it.

Out of the intelligentsia comes the spiritual leadership of the life of the state and the nation. The Hungarian national socialist state will draw from the circles of the intelligentsia the most important directive and leading organ: the national general staff. Our intelligentsia will rediscover its self respect as soon as it becomes an organic part of our national community; responsibility will fall not merely upon technical elaboration, but on the essence itself which is called upon to solve and decide some question that concerns the Nation.

We shall not educate "paperwork bureaucrats," but leaders who are responsible to the nation, even in seemingly unimportant fields. To live for paperwork is worse than death; this is why the masses of intelligentsia who were locked in offices were really living dead. They were for the greatest part letter-workers, without any of the freedom that comes from self-sufficiency or from a concrete field of action, without the least pleasure or hope of satisfying the creative instinct which slept in their strength and lived in their hearts.

Letters are dead; only the spirit of letters is life. To fight for our nation, for our people: this is the type of work from which spiritual and moral powers rise. Our intelligentsia will see that their work makes sense, and through their work, so will their lives. The intellectual will be freed from aimless accomplishments, from disillusioning uselessness, from the nightmare of impotent struggles and unfulfilled efforts which have been stifling him in the liberal past, smothering his manhood, his spirit, and his whole individuality. We are going to strengthen him spiritually and morally, so that, as he casts his eyes round the Hungarian horizon, he will be able to see clearly that the ideal for which one has to live and work is that of the people and the Fatherland. In order to fulfill its primary national function, the intelligentsia has to be nation-conscious and consciously socialist.

It should be our belief and conviction that the way shown here is the way of Hungarian life, Hungarian justice and Hungarian opportunity, but at the same time the only passable way for our other brother nations also whose existence or nonexistence is closely and inseparably tied to our moral, spiritual and material existence or nonexistence.

We shall march on this road, because we know that our Hungarian people have an important great calling which points to this road and in its aim stands the happiness, greatness and glory of our Nation.

B. SZALASI'S LAST WORDS AT HIS TRIAL, 1946

The spirit is always stronger than anyone else. If truth is the servant of life then truth will be victorious and not transient moods.

Two thousand years ago the belief of truth was on earth, but Christ was killed on the cross.

This war was not won by anyone. The purpose of war is not to knock the weapon out of the hand of the fighting party, but that the following peace should be realized on the basis of everybody's welfare and security.

I am convinced that the present events, have not yet come to a close. Neither party has conquered. The great world question, the problems which came to the surface during the war, are still unsolved.

From the point of view of the fate which lives within me and from the point of view of the new world, I always took such steps as according to my conviction were called for to serve the glory and happiness of the Hungarian Nation. . . .

On October 15, 1944, it had to be decided whether the Hungarian Nation and its leadership should move towards East or West. My decision could not be anything else, but that we must persevere; because by fighting we gain time, precious time and he who wins this time wins the war as well.

My activities had no other basis than this. It would make no sense to attribute a different reason to my decision, because I would come to total contradiction with that ideology to which I stubbornly adhere. It is not a crime that I process this with conviction. It cannot be a crime, that I could only live for this with conviction!

I do not want to exempt myself from the responsibility and I do not try to escape from it. What has been said about me is untrue and severely touches my honour.

I thank everyone without exception who has followed me on this grave road. I thank the widows, the orphans, the heroic dead, the wounded, for the sacrifices they made for this belief.

ROMANIA

A peculiar variant of National Socialism appears in Romania, in the various forms of a Christian Nationalism incarnated in a series of leagues, all led or inspired by Corneliu Codreanu.

Deeply patriotic, Codreanu saw Communism as a national challenge even more than an ideological one, for Russia lay across the border, and Romania had often figured as a pawn in her game. Deeply Christian, however, Codreanu's anti-Communism did not drive him to reaction, but to a reformist populism, which sought salvation in a change of heart as well as of economic conditions.

The passages which follow show different aspects of Codreanu's thought, different stages in his evolution and concern. All mark clearly a certain concern with purity and quality which never left him, but which many of his followers never found.

A. Corneliu Zelea Codreanu: NATIONAL CHRISTIAN SOCIALISM: FEBRUARY 9, 1920 *

The Guard of the National Conscience was a fighting organization, an organization intended to destroy the enemy.

In 1919 I often had occasion to talk with Pancu . . . and I would tell him: "It isn't enough to defeat communism we must also fight for the rights of the workers. They have a right to bread and they have a right to honour. We must fight against the oligarchic party, creating national workers organizations which can gain their rights within the framework of the State, and not against the State.

We will tolerate no one trying to raise on Romanian soil another flag than that of our national history. However right the working class might be we do not permit them to rise over and against the country's borders. You cannot, even for your bread, destroy and hand over to a foreign nation of bankers and usurers everything saved by the millenary labor of a nation of workers and heroes. Your right must be realized within the framework of your nation's right. You cannot for your right break to pieces the historic right of the nation to which you belong.

* Translated from Corneliu Zelea Codreanu, *Pentru Legionari* (Bucarest: 1936), pp. 24-26.

On the other hand we do not admit that in the shelter of tricolor formulas an oligarchic and tyrannous class should install itself on the back of workers of every kind and literally skin them, while continually appealing to the Fatherland—which they do not love, God—in whom they do not believe, Church—in which they never set foot, Army—which they send to war with empty hands.

These are realities, which cannot serve as slogans for political rackets in the hands of immoral conjurors." That is when we began to organize the workers in national syndicates and even set up a political party: "National Christian Socialism." At that time we had not heard of Adolf Hitler and of German National Socialism. Pancu then wrote:

The Creed of National Christian Socialism

I believe in one and undivided Romanian State, from the Nistru to the Tisa, including all Romanians and only Romanians, hardworking, honest, and God-fearing, ever aware of the land and its people.

Giver of equal rights, civil and political, to men and to women. Protector of the family, paying employees and workers according to the number of their children and the amount of their work, taking into consideration quantity and quality. And in a State creator of social harmony by restricting class division; and, above salaries, socializing industry—the property of all workers, and land—divided among all ploughmen.

The repartition of profits between employer (State or private) and workers. The private employer receiving, besides payment for his work, a percentage decreasing proportionately to the size of his capital. And in a State which insures the workers by a "risk fund." Founder of food and clothing stores for workers and employees who, organized in national syndicates, will be represented on the administrative committees of different industrial, agricultural, and business institutions.

And in a great and powerful "father of the workers" and King of the peasants, Ferdinand I, who for Romania's welfare has sacrificed all, and who for our salvation has become one with the people. Who was victorious at the head of the armies of Mărâşti and Mărăşeşti, who once more looks with love and trust towards the soldiers who owe him their loyalty, and who will find in the barracks a national school from which they will graduate in one year.

In a tricolor flag surrounded by the rays of National Christian Socialism, symbol of harmony between the brothers and the sisters of Greater Romania. In one Holy Christian Church with Priests who live according to the Scriptures and only for the

Scriptures, and who will sacrifice themselves apostolically for the enlightenment of the many.

I confess the election of ministers by the Chamber, the suppression of the Senate, the organization of rural police, progressive income tax, agricultural and trade schools in the villages, clubs for housewives and adults, hospices for the sick and the old, community centers, measures for determining paternity [*in cases of illegitimacy*], effective means of making the laws known to all, the encouragement of private initiative in the National interest, and the development of rural household industry.

I await the revival of national consciousness unto the last shepherd and the descent of the enlightened in the midst of the weary, to strengthen them and help them in true brotherhood, the challenge of the Romania of tomorrow. Amen.

B. Corneliu Zelea Codreanu: THE LEGION OF THE ARCHANGEL MICHAEL: OUR PROGRAM (1927)*

This group of young people was the first beginning of legionary life. It was the foundation stone. It had to be placed on solid ground.

Therefore I didn't say: Let us go and conquer Romania! Go into the villages and cry: "A new political organization has been founded, join it, all of you." I did not draw up a new *political program*, beside the other ten already existing in Romania, all of them "perfect" as far as their authors and their partisans were concerned, and I did not send legionaries to wave it around the villages, calling on men to take it up in order to save the country.

From this point of view, too, we shall be fundamentally different from all the other political organizations, and from Cuza's party. All believe that the country is dying for lack of good programs. And so they put together some perfectly congealed program and they take off with it to gather men. That is why people ask: "What program have you got?"

This country is dying for lack of *men*, not for lack of programs. That is what we think. Therefore, it is not programs we must create, *but men, new men*. Because the way men are today *overgrown with politicking* and *infected* by Jewish influence, they are bound to compromise the most brilliant programs. This kind of man, who lives today in Romanian politics, we have met him before in history. Under his rule nations have died and States have collapsed. . . .

* Translated from Corneliu Zelea Codreanu, *Pentru Legionari* (Bucarest: 1936), pp. 284-287.

If this type of man continues to lead this country the Romanian people will close its eyes forever, and Romania will collapse, in spite of all the brilliant programs with which the cunning of the degenerate [*politicians*] may fool the unhappy masses. . . .

That is why the keystone of the Legions is *man;* not the political program. The reform of man, not the reform of political programs. It follows that the Legion of the Archangel Michael will be more a school and an army than a political party. . . .

From this legionary school *a new man* must appear, a man with heroic qualities. A giant in our history, who will fight and win against all the enemies of the Fatherland, his struggle and his victory extending beyond, to the invisible enemies, to the power of evil. The finest souls that our minds can conceive, the proudest, tallest, straightest, strongest, cleverest, cleanest, bravest and most hardworking that our race can produce, this is what the legionary schools must give us! A man in which all the possibilities of human greatness that God has sown in the blood of our people should be developed to the maximum.

This hero graduated from legionary school *will also know* how to produce programs, *will also know* how to persuade the other Romanians: and if he cannot, he will know how to get his way and win, that is why he is a hero.

This hero, this representative of bravery, of labour, of justice, with the powers of God in his soul, will lead our people on the road of its greatness. . . . We shall create a spiritual atmosphere, a moral atmosphere, in which the heroic man may be born and on which he can thrive.

Such an atmosphere must be isolated from the rest of the world by the most elevated spiritual buttresses. It must be guarded against all the dangerous winds of cowardice, corruption, decadence, and of all the curses which bury nations and individuals. After the legionary has developed in this kind of atmosphere, in the Nest [*the cell*], the workcamp, in the organization and the legionary family itself, he will be sent into the world: *to live,* in order to learn how to behave properly; *to fight,* in order to learn how to be brave and strong; *to work,* in order to learn the habit of working and the love of all those who labour; *to suffer,* in order to steel himself; *to sacrifice,* in order to get used to transcending his own person in the service of his people.

Wherever he goes, he will create a new atmosphere of the same kind. He will be an example. He will make other legionaries; and people, looking for better days, will follow him.

C. WHAT A LEGIONARY BELIEVES *

#67 The State which is based on the old ideology of the French Revolution is bound for ruin. The problem the world faces is that of a new State. It could be very good or very bad. How will it be? According to how we forge it.

#68 However, the new State cannot be founded only on theoretical concepts of constitutional law. The new State presupposes in the first place and as an essential a new type of man. A new State with men with old sins is inconceivable.

#69 The new man or the renewed nation presupposes a great spiritual renewal, a great spiritual revolution of the whole people, a revolution that is opposed to the Spiritual direction of our day and an explicit offensive against this direction.

#70 In this new man all the virtues of the human soul will have to revive. All the qualities of our race. In this new man all the results of evil, all the inclinations towards evil will have to be stifled. In this new type of hero—hero in the warlike sense: so that through struggle he may impose his ideas; hero in the social sense: incapable after his victory of exploiting another's labor; hero of labor: the gigantic creator of his land by his work—must be concentrated the best that the Romanian people has gathered over thousands of years. This is the man we await, this hero, this giant. Upon him the new State, the Romania of tomorrow will be founded. Before being a political, theoretical, financial, economic movement, the Legionary Movement is a spiritual school, in which if a man shall enter, a hero must come out at the other end.

#73 Laws, martial law, bayonets which can check a nation's destiny have never existed, do not exist, and never will exist.

— Reading No. 5 —

GREAT BRITAIN

The so-called Modern Movement, launched as a Labour Party ginger group, was going to end in Fascism. By 1930, the depression had hit England hard, and England hurt. Young men

* Translated from *Cârticica şefului de cuib* (1944), pp. 87-90.

wanted to do something—anything. Old men, at least those in office, wanted to sit tight. It was from this dilemma that British Fascism grew.

Sir Oswald Mosley's career is a good illustration of the irritation of young men faced with sluggish, elderly indecision, their frustration at seeing stones thrown against Party glass-houses turning to sponges in mid-air, the narrow gap between one sort of radicalism and another, between good intentions and degrading means, between great ambitions and sordid ends.

Mosley's argument appears most cogently in this first and most successful of his propaganda works, when it had not become completely impossible to take him seriously as a would-be reformer.

✓   ✓   ✓

A. Oswald Mosley: THE MODERN MOVEMENT *

Misrepresentation. We are also faced by the fact that a few people have misused the name "Fascism" in this country, and from ignorance or in perversion have represented it as the "White Guard of reaction."

This is indeed a strange perversion of a creed of dynamic change and progress. In all countries, Fascism has been led by men who came from the "Left," and the rank and file has combined the Conservative and patriotic elements of the nation with ex-Socialists, ex-Communists and revolutionaries who have forsaken their various *illusions* of progress for the new orderly *reality* of progress. In our new organization we now combine within our ranks all those elements in this country who have long studied and understood the great constructive mission of Fascism; but we have no place for those who have sought to make Fascism the lackey of reaction, and have thereby misrepresented its policy and dissipated its strength. In fact Fascism is the greatest constructive and revolutionary creed in the world. It seeks to achieve its aim legally and constitutionally, by methods of law and order; *but in objective it is revolutionary or it is nothing.* It challenges the existing order and advances the constructive alternative of the Corporate State. To many of us this creed represents the thing which we have sought throughout our political lives. *It combines the dynamic urge to change and progress, with the authority, the discipline and the order without which nothing great can be achieved.*

The essence of Fascism is the power of adaptation to fresh facts. Above all, it is a realist creed. It has no use for immortal

* From Oswald Mosley, *The Greater Britain* (London: 1932), pp. 15-16, 149-160.

principles in relation to the facts of bread-and-butter; and it despises the windy rhetoric which ascribes importance to mere formula. The steel creed of an iron age, it cuts through the verbiage of illusion to the achievement of a new reality. . . .

Conclusion. The case advanced in these pages covers, not only a new political policy, but also a new conception of life. In our view, these purposes can only be achieved by the creation of a modern movement invading every sphere of national life. To succeed, such a movement must represent the organized revolt of the young manhood of Britain against things as they are. The enemy is the Old Gang of our present political system. No matter what their party label, the old parliamentarians have proved themselves to be all the same. . . .

It is only natural that nations in crisis should seek the easy and the normal way of escape. It is only natural that they should trust the well-known and venerable figures in politics until they are found unworthy of trust and unsuitable to a dynamic age. Only then, with the new determination born of despair, great nations turn to new forces and to new men.

The first result of crisis in every nation has always been a national combination of "the united Muttons." Only after their failure, the modern movement begins its inevitable advance. The aim of such a movement must be revolutionary in the fundamental changes which it seeks to secure. . . .

To drift much longer, to muddle through much further, is to run the risk of collapse. In such a situation, new ideas will not come peacefully; they will come violently, as they have come elsewhere. In the final economic crisis to which neglect may lead, argument, reason, persuasion, vanish, and organized force alone prevails. In such a situation, the eternal protagonists in the history of all modern crises must struggle for the mastery of the State. Either Fascism or Communism emerges victorious; if it be the latter, the story of Britain is told.

Anyone who argues that in such a situation the normal instruments of government, such as police and army, can be used effectively, has studied neither the European history of his own time nor the realities of the present situation. In the highly technical struggle for the modern State in crisis, only the technical organizations of Fascism and of Communism have ever prevailed or, in the nature of the case, can prevail. Governments and Parties which have relied on the normal instruments of government . . . have fallen easy and ignoble victims to the forces of anarchy. . . . We shall prepare to meet the anarchy of Communism with the organized force of Fascism; but we do not seek that struggle, and for the sake of the nation we desire to avert it. Only when we see the feeble surrender to menacing problems, the fatuous optimism which again and again has been disproved, the spineless drift towards disaster, do we feel it necessary to organize for such a contingency.

It is often urged strenuously upon me that I could find acceptance for many of the ideas set out in this book within one of the existing parties, and that it is folly to attempt the great labor of creating new machinery for purposes which could be achieved by existing machinery. Such an argument betrays a complete misunderstanding of the problems and the history of this period. It would have been equally futile to tell an Italian Fascist that he could achieve the renaissance of Italy through the Parliament of Giolitti, or a German Nazi that he should cease his struggle and should seek to persuade the opponents whose failure created the necessity for his organization. New ideas have never come, in the modern world, except from the new and organized reality.

In Great Britain salvation has not come, in fourteen years, from the old parties, and it will not come. They are not alive to crisis; they are not organized to meet it; and their mind and psychology are unsuited to it. We cannot compromise with them, for "their ways are not our ways and their gods are not our gods."

It is true that within the old parties and even within the old Parliament are many young men whose real place is with us, and who sympathize with our ideas. The real political division of the past decade has not been a division of parties, but a division of generations. . . . We have to discover, as we have already discovered, new men, and we have to create a new force from nothing except the will of the mass of the people to victory.

It is thus that every Fascist movement has arrived at power —not by combinations of men drawn from the old political system, but by the discovery of new men who come from nowhere, and by the creation of a new force which is free from the trammels of the past. . . .

In the coming struggle, we shall have the imposing things of the world against us, and much of its material strength. . . . But we have on our side forces which have carried such movements to victory throughout the world. *We have in unison in our cause the economic facts and the spiritual tendencies of our age.* . . . For our part, we appeal to our countrymen to take action while there is time, and to carry the changes which are necessary by the legal and constitutional methods which are available. If on the other hand every appeal to reason is futile in the future, as it has been in the immediate past, and this Empire is allowed to drift until collapse and anarchy supervene, we shall not shrink from that final conclusion, and will organize to stand between the State and ruin.

We are accused of organizing to promote violence. That accusation is untrue. It is true that we are organized to protect our meetings as far as possible from violence, and very necessary that organization has proved in practice. Already in this country we have a condition in which free speech is a thing of the past. The leaders of the old political parties creep in by back doors, under police protection, to well-ticketed meetings which would otherwise be broken up by the organized violence of Socialist and Communist extremists. We have thrown open our meetings to the public, and after the meetings we have exercised the Englishman's right to walk through the streets of our great cities. When we have been attacked, we have hit back. . . . When we are confronted by red terror, we are certainly organized to meet force by force, and will always do our utmost to smash it. We shall continue to exercise the right of free speech, and will do our utmost to defend it. Emphatically, this does not mean that we seek violence. On the contrary, we seek our aims by methods which are both legal and constitutional, and we appeal to our country by taking action in time to avert the possibility of violence. If the situation of violence is to be averted, the Old Gang Government must be overthrown and effective measures must be adopted before the situation has gone too far. The enemy today is the Old Gang of present parliamentarism. The enemy of tomorrow, if their rule persists much longer, will be the Communist Party. *The Old Gang are the architects of disaster, the Communists only its executors.* Not until the Old Gangs have muddled us to catastrophe can Communists really operate; so, in the first place, the enemy is the Old Gang, and the objective is the overthrow of their power. To achieve this by constitutional means will entail at a later stage a bid for parliamentary power. In a superficial paradox, it will be necessary for a modern movement which does not believe in Parliament, as at present constituted, to seek to capture Parliament. To us Parliament will never be an end in itself, but only a means to an end; our object is, not political place-holding, but the achievement of national reconstruction.

However, the time for elections and Parliament has not yet come. First, it is necessary to build a movement invading every phase of national life and carrying everywhere the Corporate conception. In the first instance, we probably made a mistake in contesting parliamentary elections before we had created such a machine. It is a mistake which we have made in common with all new movements which have come to power in Europe since the War. In all cases the phase of ridicule and defeat has to be passed; indeed, it is the test of a movement's vitality. In the beginning the Old Gangs carry the day—as lightheartedly as Remus leapt over the half built walls of Rome.

Whether our British Union of Fascist Parties will arrive at power through the parliamentary system, or whether it will reach power in a situation far beyond the control of Parliament, no one can tell. The solution of that question will depend on two incalculable factors: 1) the rapidity with which the situation degenerates; 2) the rapidity with which the British people accept the necessity for new forms and for new *organizations*. If the situation develops rapidly, and the public mind develops slowly, something like collapse may come before any new movement has captured parliamentary power.

In that case, other and sterner measures must be adopted for the saving of a State in a situation approaching anarchy. Such a situation will be none of our seeking. In no case shall we resort to violence against the forces of the Crown; but only against the forces of anarchy if, and when, the machinery of state has been allowed to drift into powerlessness. Strangely enough, such an eventuality is probably a lesser menace, when the character of the British people is considered, than the possibility of a long, slow decline which is so imperceptible that the national will to action is not aroused. In crisis the British are at their best; when the necessity for action is not clear, they are at their worst. It is possible that we may not come to any clearly marked crisis: and here arises a still greater danger. The industrial machine is running on two cylinders instead of six. A complete breakdown would be a stronger incentive to action than the movement, however cumbrous, of a crippled machine. So long as there is movement of any kind, however inadequate, there is always a lazy hope of better things. The supreme danger is that Britain may sink, almost in her sleep, to the position of a Spain—alive, in a sense, but dead to all sense of greatness and to her mission in the world.

In a situation of so many and such diverse contingencies, nobody can dogmatise upon the future. We cannot say with certainty when catastrophe will come, nor whether it will take the form of a sharp crisis or of a steady decline to the status of a second-rate Power. All that we can say with certainty is that Britain cannot muddle on much longer without catastrophe, or the loss of her position in the world. Against either contingency it is our duty to arouse the nation. To meet either the normal situation of political action, or the abnormal situation of catastrophe, it is our duty to organize. Therefore, while the principles for which we fight can be clearly described in a comprehensive system of politics, of economics and of life, it would be folly to describe precisely in advance the road by which we shall attain them. A great man of action once observed: "No man goes very far who knows exactly where he is going," and the same observation applies with some force to modern movements of reality in the changing situations of today.

We ask those who join us to march with us in a great and hazardous adventure. We ask them to be prepared to sacrifice all, but to do so for no small and unworthy ends. We ask them to dedicate their lives to building in this country a movement of the modern age, which, by its British expression will transcend, as often before in our history, every precursor of the Continent in conception and in constructive achievement.

We ask them to rewrite the greatest pages of British history by finding for the spirit of their age its highest mission in these islands. Neither to our friends nor to the country do we make any promises; not without struggle and ordeal will the future be won. Those who march with us will certainly face abuse, misunderstanding, bitter animosity, and possibly the ferocity of struggle and danger. In return, we can only offer to them the deep belief that they are fighting that a great land may live.

— Reading No. 6 —

SPAIN

The best-known and most attractive representative of Falangism was José Antonio Primo de Rivera. Though his works have not been translated, long excerpts from his speeches appear in Stanley Payne's excellent Falange. *In the following passage, the rise of Socialism is explained by the economic slavery that liberalism imposes, and the workers' social claims are accepted as long as they do not threaten the unity and the being of the Fatherland.*

✓   ✓   ✓

A. José Antonio Primo de Rivera:
WHAT THE FALANGE WANTS *

Finally, the liberal state came to offer us economic slavery, saying to the workers, with tragic sarcasm: "You are free to

* From his Madrid speech of October 29, 1933, translated by Stanley G. Payne, *Falange* (Stanford: 1961), pp. 38-41. By permission of Stanford University Press.

work as you wish; no one can compel you to accept specified conditions. Since we are the rich, we offer you the conditions that please us; as free citizens, you are not obliged to accept them if you do not want to; but as poor citizens, if you do not accept them you will die of hunger, surrounded of course by the utmost liberal dignity." . . .

Therefore socialism had to appear, and its coming was just (for we do not deny any evident truth). The workers had to defend themselves against a system that only promised them right and did not strive to give them a just life. However, socialism, which was a legitimate reaction against liberal slavery, went astray because it resulted, first, in the materialist interpretation of life and history; second, in a sense of reprisal; and third, in the proclamation of the dogma of class struggle. . . .

The Patria is a total unity, in which all individuals and classes are integrated; the Patria cannot be in the hands of the strongest class or of the best organized party. The Patria is a transcendent synthesis, an indivisible synthesis, with its own goals to fulfill; and we want this movement of today, and the state which it creates, to be an efficient, authoritarian instrument at the service of an indisputable unity, of that permanent unity, of that irrevocable unity that is the Patria.

And we already have the principle for our future acts and our present conduct, for we would be just another party if we came to announce a program of concrete solutions. Such programs have the advantage of never being fulfilled.

Here is what is required by our total sense of the Patria and the state which is to serve it:

That all the people of Spain, however diverse they may be, feel in harmony with an irrevocable unity of destiny.

That the political parties disappear. No one was ever born a member of a political party; on the other hand, we are all born members of a family; we are all neighbors in a municipality; we all labor in the exercise of a profession . . . .

We want less liberal word-mongering and more respect for the deeper liberty of man. For one respects the liberty of man when he is esteemed, as we esteem him, the bearer of eternal values; when he is esteemed as the corporal substance of a soul capable of being damned and of being saved. Only when man is considered thus can it truly be said that his liberty is respected, and more especially if that liberty is joined, as we aspire to join it, to a system of authority, of hierarchy, and of order. . . .

Finally, we desire that if on some occasion this must be achieved by violence, there be no shrinking from violence. Because who has said—while speaking of "everything save violence"—that the supreme value in the hierarchy of values is amiability? Who has said that when our sentiments are insulted we are obliged to be accommodating instead of reacting like men? It is very correct indeed that dialectic is the first instrument of communication. But no other dialectic is admissible save the dialectic of fists and pistols when justice or the Patria is offended. . . .

But our movement would not be understood at all if it were believed to be only a manner of thinking. It is not a manner of thinking; it is a manner of being. We ought not merely to propose to ourselves a formal construction, a political architecture. Before life in its entirety, in each one of our acts, we must adopt a complete, profound, and human attitude. This attitude is the spirit of sacrifice and service, the ascetic and military sense of life. Henceforth let no one think that we recruit men in order to offer rewards; let no one imagine that we join together in the defense of privileges. I should like to have this microphone before me carry my voice into every last working-class home to say: Yes, we wear a tie; yes, you may say of us that we are *señoritos*. But we urge a spirit of struggle for things that cannot concern us as *señoritos;* we come to fight so that hard and just sacrifices may be imposed on many of our own class, and we come to struggle for a totalitarian state that can reach the humble as well as the powerful with its benefits. We are thus, for so always in our history have been the *señoritos* of Spain. In this manner they have achieved the true status of *señores,* because in distant lands, and in our very Patria, they have learned to suffer death and to carry out hard missions precisely for reasons in which, as *señoritos,* they had no interest at all.

I believe the banner is raised. Now we are going to defend it gaily, poetically. There are some who think that in order to unite men's wills against the march of the revolution it is proper to offer superficially gratifying solutions; they think it is necessary to hide everything in their propaganda which could awaken an emotion or signify energetic or extreme action. What equivocation! The peoples have never been moved by anyone save the poets, and woe to him who, before the poetry which destroys, does not know how to raise the poetry which promises!

In a poetic movement we shall raise this fervent feeling for Spain; we shall sacrifice ourselves; we shall renounce ourselves, and the triumph will be ours, a triumph—why need I say it?— that we are not going to win in the next elections. In those elections vote for whoever seems to you least undesirable. But our Spain will not emerge from [*the Cortes*], nor is our goal there. The atmosphere there is tired and murky, like a tavern

at the end of a night of dissipation. That is not our place.
Yes, I know that I am a candidate; but I am one without faith
and without respect. I say this now, when it can mean that
I lose votes. That matters not at all. We are not going to
argue with habitués over the disordered remains of a dirty
banquet. Our place is outside, though we may occasionally
have to pass a few transient minutes within. Our place is in
the fresh air, under the cloudless heavens, weapons in our
hands, with the stars above us. Let the others go on with their
merrymaking. We outside, in tense, fervent, and certain vigi-
lance, already feel the dawn breaking in the joy of our hearts.

— Reading No. 7 —

BELGIUM

*The Belgium of the 1930's knew two kinds of Nationalism:
that of the Flemish, who sought a form of national self-determination and tried to affirm their rights over the French-speak-
ing Walloons, but whose particularist Nationalism belongs to
an older tradition with no social implications; and that of the
Social Nationalism of Rex.*

*We may follow, below, the evolution of Rex, from its origins
as a Catholic youth movement, to its sudden emergence as an
anti-party party in 1936. And we may judge the populist—
and popular—appeal of Léon Degrelle, the movement's youthful, demagogic leader, who oscillates between a very Belgian
rejection of violence and a highly emotional (and typically
Fascist) demand for his followers' souls.*

1   1   1

A. Jean Denis:
THE FUNDAMENTALS OF REXIST DOCTRINE *

1. REX IS NEITHER A PARTY NOR A LEAGUE
Rex is a *movement,* that is to say an active force carrying
a current of ideas.

* Jean Denis, *Bases Doctrinales de Rex* (Brussels: 1936),
pp. 8-11.

Rex is a *revolutionary* movement.

Rex is a *popular* movement.

The Rexist movement wants:

(a) *the destruction of the parties* which have arbitrarily divided the citizenry, consigning the nation to disorder, to extortions and to the uncontrolled rule of politicians ruled themselves by an anonymous oligarchy. This anonymous oligarchy, made up of those who really hold all powers in the country, manoeuvres in the shadows. It sways the vast herd of proletarianized citizens of all social classes, and, on the other hand, holds at its mercy, by their stupidity and by their cupidity, the country's political leadership. This anonymous oligarchy constitutes the only permanent and united force over against the bickering, squabbling parties, which have never been as rotten or as contemptible as they are today.

(b) *the reconstruction of a popular community* established on elementary moral foundations accepted by all. This popular community, Rex has started by restoring it within its own ranks. Within Rex and around Rex gather the men of *all* parties who understand that this regime is rotten, decaying, and that it must be replaced by something else—something lively, active, and capable of progress and of growth.

2. THE POPULAR COMMUNITY

The concept of the *individual* which forms the erroneous philosophical foundation of the present regime, and which was born of the catastrophic ideologies of the 17th and 18th centuries, must be replaced by the concept of the *human being*, which corresponds exactly to the reality of man—a social being endowed with a fundamental dignity, which society can help develop, and with which it has no right to interfere. The human being thrives not by referring everything to itself in a vain and selfish individualism but, on the contrary, by giving up the self and becoming part of communities.

The first community in which the human being thrives is the *family*.

The second community in which the human being thrives is the *profession*.

The third community in which the human being thrives is the *cultural and linguistic community*.

The fourth community in which the human being thrives is the *national community*.

All these communities combined constitute the *popular community*.

The State must serve the popular community.

The role of the State is to serve the common weal, by maintaining *peace among the citizens,* and by promoting *public prosperity.* The role of the State is to *direct, survey, stimulate, or curb,* according to circumstances or to necessity. The role of the State is not *to substitute itself to particular communities,* much better fitted than it is to see that human beings flourish. By taking the place of particular communities, the State has ruined, destroyed, annihilated them and thus handed over, unprotected, the liberties and rights of the weak to the bad faith of the strong and sly.

The Rexist movement wants:

(a) the destruction of all that which in the present regime compromises the existence of particular communities, suppresses their dignity—that is their functions and their social responsibilities. The congestion of the State must be relieved, so that it can carry out the functions peculiar to it more freely, more forcefully and more effectively.

(b) the reconstruction of particular communities, by a comprehensive series of measures designed to restore their position, their rights and their duties in the aggregate of the popular community. THIS IS WHY THE PROGRAM OF REX IS FAMILIAL, PROFESSIONAL, CULTURAL AND LINGUISTIC, NATIONAL.

The political regime under which we live recognizes neither the existence nor the rights of the family, the profession, or the cultural and linguistic community; it has lost even the concept of national community, which has been replaced by the contest of private interests.

We may well say that *what we need is no more nor less than a revolution,* that is: to change the shape of things and re-create natural hierarchies indispensable to the welfare of man, which would be *the revolution of order.* A revolution directed against a well-ordered state of things is a revolution of disorder. Our revolution against a disorderly state of things is a revolution of order.

3. GENERAL OBJECTIVES OF THE REXIST REVOLUTION

Our first and essential goal is to *re-create and to re-establish* in their lost dignity the particular communities in which the human personality will be free to flourish. These communities are not based exclusively upon material interests. *They are, above all, of a moral nature.* But we believe that the moral order conditions all the others, and that even purely economic questions are above all social.

Before dealing with particular questions which interest a minority of people, it is necessary to consider the general questions which concern everybody. What we want is, first PEACE, then PROSPERITY.

Alone, and overly congested, before isolated individuals left to themselves, the State, as it exists at present, has shown itself incapable of ensuring either prosperity or peace. To secure peace and prosperity for all, we must begin by ensuring it—and, first and foremost by ensuring existence and dignity—to Families, to Professions, to Cultural and Linguistic Communities, to the National Community.

B. Léon Degrelle: THE MESSAGE OF REX *

All the past of the Belgian people, all our sensitiveness, all our national life, go against a regime of violence and terror. To affirm that Rex wants a dictatorship is a hateful lie against which we rise with all our heart and all our strength. Does the fact of having a leader imply dictatorship? There are, in that case, a great many dictators, from the leader of industry and the school principal to the head-cook. Dictatorship, as the mass of the people understands it, means the brutal, liberticide and uncontrolled rule of a people and a country. Rex will fight such a regime with all its power. But opposition to tyranny does not mean rejection of all authority. Authority may be necessary and beneficial. It must be based entirely upon a spontaneous trust. The Rexist State will be no more authoritarian than our movement is: the only disciplines it will establish will be based on the need to ensure cohesion of common endeavor. The Leader, in Rex, is the one who sees in the nation, at all levels, not slaves or robots, but collaborators in a common task. The people has sought in vain these last fifteen years to make its voice heard, to say what it wanted, to learn what was wanted of it. But there is a divorce between people and power.

By going to the masses, by reaching millions of readers, by gathering immense crowds, we of Rex have wanted to cast from one shore to the other, across the empty gap, the arches whose span will tomorrow unite the nation and our popular power.

We are the true democrats.

We advance only carried by the will of the people. It is the people alone who will bring us to power. It is the people alone who will maintain us there. . . . No regime will ever base itself as much as ours upon the incessant adherence of the people. We shall multiply the contacts with it, over the air, on the screen, by mass meetings, by a truly truly total universal suffrage, and by means of popular referendums. Our regime will be strong, coherent, constructive, because it will be built upon the rock: upon the people. . . .

Rex is the realm of total souls, which do not bargain, which

* Quoted by Jacques Saint-Germain, *La Bataille de Rex* (Paris: 1937), pp. 210-214, 216-218.

march straight ahead, certain of the road. This is the true
Rexist miracle; this faith, this unspoilt, burning confidence,
this complete lack of selfishness and individualism, this tension
of the whole being towards the service—however ungrateful,
no matter where, no matter how—of a cause which transcends
the individual, demanding all, promising nothing.

In a century when people live only for themselves, Rex has
taught hundreds and thousands of men to live no longer for
themselves but for a political ideal, to consent for its sake and
in advance to every sacrifice, every humiliation, every kind of
heroism.

— Reading No. 8 —

FRANCE

*Georges Valois' Faisceau was born in 1925, under the direct
influence of Mussolini's fascios, and while memories of the
hopes, the comradeship, and the confidence of 1914-1918 still
lived. It was a movement of ex-servicemen who wanted a
world fit for heroes to live in. After 1926, the brief interlude
between the treaty of Locarno and the great depression killed
it, by making both peace and prosperity seem attainable without drastic effort.*

*At the other extreme, and perhaps as a result of such laziness
of the mind and will, we find the National Popular Rally or
R.N.P.: a Socialist-Collaborationist group of the forties, set up
in German-occupied Paris by a group of veteran Socialists. In
the platform he outlines below, Marcel Déat tries to reconcile
anti-Communism and anti-capitalism with the ethnic collectivism his Nazi masters impose, and with a strong call for European unity. Momentary pressures had turned national into
international Socialists, and gathered around the same losing
cause the collectivistic partisans of international organization
and the chauvinistic prophets of national self-affirmation.*

1   1   1

A. Georges Valois: WHAT IS FASCISM? *

A European Historical Necessity. Fascism absorbs and goes beyond liberalism, democracy and Socialism. Just as, whether monarchy or republic, the modern State will be Fascist, that is, non-parliamentary, unitary, and syndical.

The birth of Fascism has opened a great debate in [*France*]. We shall not enter it. Fascism is both movement and ideas. Its worth will be proved by what it does. We limit ourselves to an explanatory statement concerning the doctrines and methods of Fascism.

There is little to say on the question whether Fascism is peculiarly Italian: here too, only the results of action will tell. If Fascism succeeds in Europe, no one will gainsay that it is European. Going by what one can see in every European country, Fascism is the name given to the movement by which modern nations seek to break the framework of old parties, break out of the parliamentary matrix and create the modern State.

Senator Enrico Corradini has recently furnished one of the best definitions of Fascism. Corradini insists that Fascism is not a reaction, demanding a return to an earlier political situation, but the outcome of historical development, "The Fascist regime," says Corradini, "is born when, historically, as in Italy, it had to take over from the old liberalism—and in this sense one can say that it is liberal—and that it came to go beyond the old liberalism—and in this sense it is antiliberal. Fascism arises to take the succession of the old democracy and go beyond it, as it took the succession of Socialism and went beyond it. Fascism, in fact, has been the great unifying national political movement whch answered historical necessity."

We shall retain this excellent definition, which shows Fascism absorbing and outstripping democracy and Socialism, and carrying into effect that which was most useful about these two movements. It is in this sense that Fascism has a European (not merely a purely local character).

This is true to such an extent that in all countries and in almost all parties Fascist tendencies show themselves. All parties have been divided by the war. Each party has a parliamentary group and an anti-parliamentary and syndicalist group. And while parliamentary groups continue to oppose each other according to the old party spirit, the anti-parliamentary and syndicalist groups of all parties attempt to get together in order to act together, according to the unitary

* From *Le Nouveau Siècle*, December 13, 1925.

spirit of the *faisceau*. The men who represent anti-parliamentary and syndicalist groups feel at one in spite of the party labels they still wear, and far from the old representatives of their own parties.

The foundation of the Club Camille Desmoulins by Pierre Dominique, furnishes a particularly strong proof of this. Republican, War veteran, with the feelings of the men of 1791, Jacobin, and ready to defend the Republic arms in hand, Pierre Dominique founds the Club Camille Desmoulins according to the purest Fascist spirit, with the following program:

1. Immediate dissolution of Parliament;
2. Turning over Power to a small group of men who would take all initiatives and all responsibility, and operate as a Committee of Public Safety;
3. Organization of specialist Ministries, the Minister himself being a Specialist under the orders of the Committee of Public Safety;
4. Early convention of Estates General.

This new organization of the Republic should aim at the following reforms:

1. Broad financial reform;
2. Setting up syndical organization;
3. Administrative reform with regionalist tendencies;
4. Absolute religious toleration, France being considered a Positivist Republic;
5. Improvement of the lot of workers and veterans by completely new legislation.

Here is a program very close to ours. In the letter—and in the spirit, for the spirit which moves the Club Camille Desmoulins is that of the war veterans: "It is our generation and no other which, from 1914 to 1918, when all seemed lost and only honor could still be saved, saved all. It is this generation, too, which, supported by its juniors, will save the French nation and give it the organizing State, guardian of the laws, which it needs."

I do not know what conventional Republicans will think of Pierre Dominique's words. But one can say with certainty that his conceptions will get the better of Parliament's outworn rubbish. Parliamentarism, the representation of different opinions, the division of the nation into parties, all these are completely out-of-date. The Parliamentary State is about as useful as an ox-cart compared to an automobile.

In the 19th century, republicans, royalists, Socialists were parliamentary and, whether under the Republican or the monarchist label, all European States became parliamentary regimes. In the 20th century, the young generations, whether republican, royalist, or Socialist, are anti-parliamentary, unitary and syndicalist. Before ten years have passed, all European states, whatever they call themselves, will be unitary, syndicalist, in one word, Fascist.

Fascism is, as Corradini points out, the movement by which Europe will absorb and transcend all democratic and Socialist experiments, and will create the modern State endowed with indispensable economic structures and capable of giving the economic forces of the modern world the national and social discipline which will make them beneficial.

B. Marcel Déat: WHAT THE R.N.P. WANTS *

1. A France which shall save its unity and its future by fulfilling its European duty against the evils of bolshevism and of capitalism.

2. A France which takes a full-spirited part in the building of a solidary Community of European nations.

3. A Government determined upon this break with the past and this reconstruction, and whose internal policy is connected with that of European socialism.

4. A popular and authoritarian State, which would be—as the liberal and parliamentary State never was—the highest expression of national interest and of the French Community, and before which selfishness, privilege and feudalisms would give way.

5. A single People's Party to support, drive and control the revolutionary effort of the new State, propel the masses, assemble Youth, and make mutual social aid, from the cradle to the grave, the first task of the National Community.

6. The immediate punishment of civilians and of military responsible for war and for defeat, the revision of injustices committed since July 1940, and the prosecution of unpunished offences.

7. The widest tolerance for all religious beliefs; churches and philosophic sects absolutely prohibited from all direct or indirect political activity, or from usurping in any way the educational function of the State, to which the political and civic formation of children and of youth belongs, and which owes each child a trade, an education and an ideal.

8. Defense of the French ethnic Community against unassimilable or noxious racial elements, by measures of physiological, economic and political protection, and its regeneration by ambitious policies for Youth, Sport, Public Health and the Family.

* From Marcel Déat, *Un parti, un chef* (Paris: 1943), pp. 29-32.

9. Destruction of the power of trusts and suppression of speculative profits.

10. State control of currency, credit and prices.

11. Salaries which never fail to ensure the highest living standard compatible with an indefinitely progressive level of national productivity.

12. Organization of corporative committees where Labor will have a preponderant place, where the interests of all Producers will be safeguarded, where the legitimate authority of the Manager (*Chef d'entreprise*) will be respected, and where the working class would know no limits to its social ascent than those of its merit and its capacities.

13. A powerfully equipped Agriculture, capable of a production level matching European needs, and which would know at last, through security of sales at stable and remunerative prices, normal conditions of existence.

14. A supply policy ensuring the equitable distribution of essential goods, avoiding the superfluous controls of impotent Statism, and suppressing the anarchic liberalism of the Black Market, thanks to the regulation of market prices at a normal rate of profit and to the direct cooperation of producers, carriers, distributors and consumers.

15. Work for all elements of economic life, including the middle classes and the intellectual and liberal professions.

16. Absolute protection of the rights of prisoners, veterans and victims of the war. The Community to assume responsibility for all elements that can take no part in production, but whose right to life cannot be questioned.

BRIEF BIBLIOGRAPHY

Few books in English deal directly with the events that concern us. The bibliography of the German and Italian movements is lengthy and unsatisfactory; that for Belgium and Romania is non-existent (it is best there to read the books of Codreanu and Degrelle). Those interested in exploring the question further might begin with Hannah Arendt, *The Origins of Totalitarianism* (New York: 1958); Robert Byrnes, *Anti-Semitism in Modern France* (New Brunswick: 1950); Hans Kohn, *The Idea of Nationalism* (New York: 1943); and Ernst Nolte, *Der Faschismus in seiner Epoche* (Munich: 1963), soon to be published in an American translation. If they feel somewhat confused by the different points of view, they had better remember that confusion is the essence of historical reality.

On the different countries that have been mentioned, again there are few publications available in English. For Germany, the best are Alan Bullock, *Hitler—A Study in Tyranny* (New York: 1952), and Andrew G. Whiteside, "The Nature and Origins of National Socialism," in the *Journal of Central European Affairs*, vol. XVII (1957-58), pp. 48-73. These may be supplemented by Theodore Abel, *Why Hitler Came Into Power* (New York: 1938), and Milton Mayer, *They Thought They Were Free: The Germans, 1933-45* (Chicago: 1955). On Italy, we have Denis Mack Smith, *Italy* (Ann Arbor: 1959), Dante L. Germino, *The Italian Fascist Party in Power* (Minneapolis: 1959), and Federico Chabod's beautifully clear and brief *Italia Contemporanea, 1918-48* (Turin: 1961). The English movements are presented in James Drennan, *B.U.F.: Oswald Mosley and British Fascism* (London: 1934), and Colin Cross, *The Fascists in Britain* (London: 1961). Two good books have recently been devoted to Spanish Fascism: Stanley Payne, *Falange* (Stanford: 1961), and Bernd Nellessen, *Die verbotene Revolution:*

Aufstieg und Niedergang der Falange (Hamburg: 1963). Istvan Déak's M.A. thesis, *National Socialism in Hungary* (Columbia, N.Y.: n.d.), becomes accessible in the chapter he contributes to *The Right: A Historical Profile,* edited by Hans Rogger and Eugen Weber (Berkeley: 1964). The student of contemporary Hungary must, however, consult C. A. Macartney's monumental *History of Modern Hungary, 1929-45,* 2 vols. (Edinburgh: 1956). For France, see E. Weber, *Action Française* (Stanford: 1962), and, more broadly, J. Plumyène and R. Lasierra, *Les Fascismes français* (Paris: 1963).

Most illuminating, however, are the writings of leaders and militants themselves. Their very vagueness and occasional incoherence can help to explain the nature of their appeal.

INDEX

ISLAM AND THE WEST—Hitti